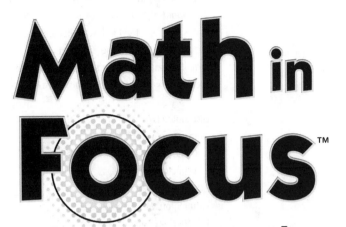

Math in Focus™

Singapore Math
by Marshall Cavendish

Reteach
5B

Author
Dr Fong Ho Kheong

Marshall Cavendish
Education

GReaT★
SOURCE®
HOUGHTON MIFFLIN HARCOURT
Supplemental Publishers

© 2009 Marshall Cavendish International (Singapore) Private Limited

Published by Marshall Cavendish Education
An imprint of Marshall Cavendish International (Singapore) Private Limited
Times Centre, 1 New Industrial Road, Singapore 536196
Customer Service Hotline: (65) 6411 0820
E-mail: tmesales@sg.marshallcavendish.com
Website: www.marshallcavendish.com/education

Distributed by
Great Source
A division of Houghton Mifflin Harcourt Publishing Company
181 Ballardvale Street
P.O. Box 7050
Wilmington, MA 01887-7050
Tel: 1-800-289-4490
Website: www.greatsource.com

First published 2009
Reprinted 2010, 2011

Math in Focus Reteach 5B
ISBN 978-0-669-01595-9

Printed in United States of America

3 4 5 6 7 8   1897   16 15 14 13 12 11
4500279300   B C D E

Contents

Introducing

Math in Focus™

Reteach

Reteach 5A and *5B*, written to complement *Math in Focus™: Singapore Math by Marshall Cavendish* Grade 5, offer a second opportunity to practice skills and concepts at the entry level. Key vocabulary terms are explained in context, complemented by sample problems with clearly worked solutions.

Not all children are able to master a new concept or skill after the first practice. A second opportunity to practice at the same level before moving on can be key to long-term success.

Monitor students' levels of understanding during daily instruction and as they work on Practice exercises. Provide *Reteach* worksheets to struggling students who would benefit from further practice at a basic level.

BLANK

CHAPTER

8 **Decimals**

Worksheet 1   Understanding Thousandths

Write the decimal shown by each arrow.

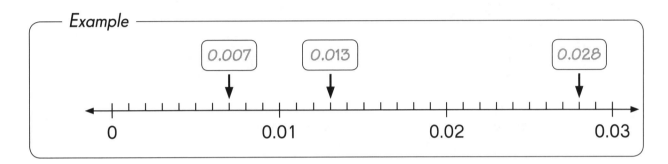

Example

| 0.007 | 0.013 | | 0.028 |

0   0.01   0.02   0.03

1.

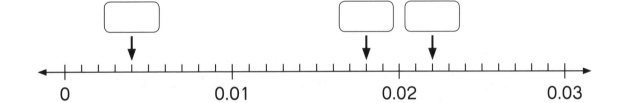

0   0.01   0.02   0.03

Find the decimal that the shaded part represents.

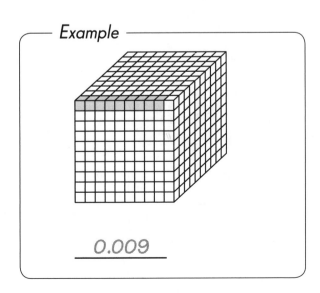

Example

_0.009_

2.

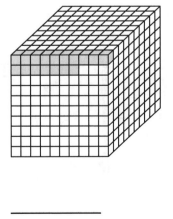

_____

Shade the correct number of cubes to show each decimal.

3.   0.004

4.   0.028

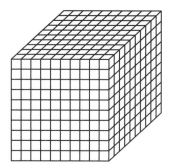

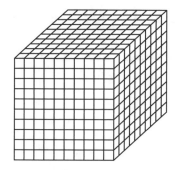

Complete the place-value chart to show the decimal.

Example

0.016

Ones		Tenths	Hundredths	Thousandths
			◯	◯ ◯ ◯ ◯ ◯ ◯

5.   0.258

Ones		Tenths	Hundredths	Thousandths

Write the decimal shown in the place-value chart.

Example

Ones		Tenths	Hundredths	Thousandths
	●		○○○	○○○○

_0.034_

6.

Ones		Tenths	Hundredths	Thousandths
○	●	○○○○	○○	○○○

_____

Complete.

Example

33 hundredths = 3 tenths _____3_____ hundredths

7.   70 thousandths = _____ hundredths

8.   5 tenths 4 hundredths = _____ thousandths

9.   6 hundredths = _____ thousandths

10.   375 thousandths = _____ hundredths _____ thousandths

Name: _____   **Date:** _____

Complete.

Example

4 hundredths 9 thousandths = _____0.049_____

---

11.   10 hundredths 7 thousandths = _____

12.   2 hundredths 15 thousandths = _____

13.   38 hundredths 13 thousandths = _____

14.   3 hundredths 8 thousandths = _____

Write each fraction as a decimal.

Example

$\dfrac{16}{1000}$ = _____0.016_____

$\dfrac{16}{1000}$ is equivalent to 0.016.

---

15. $\dfrac{7}{1000}$ = _____

16. $\dfrac{219}{1000}$ = _____

17. $\dfrac{35}{1000}$ = _____

18. $\dfrac{1476}{1000}$ = _____

Write each mixed number as a decimal.

> *Example*
>
> $3\frac{16}{1000} =$ _3.016_

19. $2\frac{5}{1000} =$ _____

20. $4\frac{391}{1000} =$ _____

21. $3\frac{56}{1000} =$ _____

22. $1\frac{108}{1000} =$ _____

**4.052 can be written in expanded form as 4 ones and 0 tenths
5 hundredths 2 thousandths.
Write each decimal in expanded notation.**

23. 2.815 = _____ ones and _____ tenths _____ hundredth

_____ thousandths

24. 2.409 = _____ ones and _____ tenths _____ hundredths

_____ thousandths

25. 7.093 = _____ ones and _____ tenths _____ hundredths

_____ thousandths

6.359 can be written in expanded form as 6 + 0.3 + 0.05 + 0.009. Write each decimal in expanded notation.

26. 4.273 = _____ + _____ + _____ + _____

27. 1.503 = _____ + _____ + _____

28. 9.017 = _____ + _____ + _____

2.478 can be written in expanded form as $2 + \dfrac{4}{10} + \dfrac{7}{100} + \dfrac{8}{1000}$. Write each decimal in expanded notation.

29. $3.165 = 3 + \dfrac{\Box}{10} + \dfrac{\Box}{100} + \dfrac{\Box}{1000}$

30. $5.294 = \underline{\hspace{2cm}} + \dfrac{2}{\Box} + \dfrac{9}{\Box} + \dfrac{4}{\Box}$

31. $4.758 = \underline{\hspace{2cm}} + \dfrac{\Box}{10} + \dfrac{5}{\Box} + \dfrac{\Box}{1000}$

32. $6.094 = \underline{\hspace{2cm}} + \dfrac{\Box}{100} + \dfrac{4}{\Box}$

33. $7.506 = \underline{\hspace{2cm}} + \dfrac{\Box}{10} + \dfrac{\Box}{\Box}$

© 2009 Marshall Cavendish International (Singapore) Private Limited. Copying is permitted; see page ii.

Fill in the blanks.

In 4.702:

34. The digit 7 is in the _____ place.

35. The digit 4 is in the _____ place.

36. The digit 2 is in the _____ place.

37. The digit 0 is in the _____ place.

In 6.908:

38. The value of the digit 9 is _____.

39. The value of the digit 0 is _____.

40. The value of the digit 8 is _____.

41. The value of the digit 6 is _____.

In 7.035:

42. The digit 3 stands for _____.

43. The digit 0 is in the _____ place.

44. The digit 5 is in the _____ place.

45. The value of the digit 7 is _____.

Solve.

46.   The digit 9 stands for 9 ones.
The digit 7 is in the tenths place.
The value of the digit 4 is 0.04.
The digit 2 is in the thousandths place.
What is the decimal?

47.   The value of the digit 8 is 0.8.
The digit 1 stands for 1 hundredth.
The digit 5 is in the ones place.
The value of the digit 4 is 0.004.
Find the decimal.

Worksheet 2   Comparing and Rounding Decimals

Use the place-value chart to compare the decimals.
Which decimal is greater?

Example

	Ones	Tenths	Hundredths	Thousandths
0.054	0	0	5	4
0.54	0	5	4	0

Compare the ones. Are they the same?   Yes / No ____Yes____

Compare the tenths. Are they the same?   Yes / No ____No____

____5____ tenths > ____0____ tenths

____0.54____ is greater than ____0.054____.

1.

	Ones	Tenths	Hundredths	Thousandths
0.108				
0.12				

Compare the ones. Are they the same?   Yes / No _____

Compare the tenths. Are they the same?   Yes / No _____

Compare the hundredths. Are they the same?   Yes / No _____

_____ hundredths > _____ hundredths

_____ is greater than _____.

Write the greater decimal.

2.   3.4 or 3.9 _____

3.   16.23 or 16.71 _____

4.   105.67 or 105.01 _____

5.   3.03 or 3.19 _____

6.   99.89 or 98.98 _____

7.   0.859 or 0.891 _____

8.   133.2 or 132.0 _____

Use the place-value chart to compare the decimals. Which decimal is the least?

Example

	Ones	Tenths	Hundredths	Thousandths
2.375	2	3	7	5
2.357	2	3	5	7
2.385	2	3	8	5

Compare the ones. Are they the same?   Yes / No   _Yes_

Compare the tenths. Are they the same?   Yes / No   _Yes_

Compare the hundredths. Are they the same?   Yes / No   _No_

___8___ hundredths > ___7___ hundredths > ___5___ hundredths

The least decimal is ___2.357___.

9.

	Ones	Tenths	Hundredths	Thousandths
4.857				
4.852				
4.854				

Compare the ones. Are they the same?   Yes / No _____

Compare the tenths. Are they the same?   Yes / No _____

Compare the hundredths. Are they the same?   Yes / No _____

Compare the thousandths. Are they the same?   Yes / No _____

_____ thousandths > _____ thousandths > _____ thousandths

The least decimal is _____.

Use the place-value chart to compare the decimals. Which decimal is the greatest?

— *Example* —

	Ones	Tenths	Hundredths
3.17	3	1	7
3.08	3	0	8
3.42	3	4	2

Compare the ones. Are they the same?   Yes / No ___Yes___

Compare the tenths. Are they the same?   Yes / No ___No___

___4___ tenths > ___1___ tenth > ___0___ tenths

The greatest decimal is ___3.42___.

10.

	Ones	Tenths	Hundredths	Thousandths
5.273				
5.291				
5.248				

Compare the ones. Are they the same?   Yes / No _____

Compare the tenths. Are they the same?   Yes / No _____

Compare the hundredths. Are they the same?   Yes / No _____

_____ hundredths > _____ hundredths > _____ hundredths

The greatest decimal is _____.

Cross out the greatest decimal and circle the least.

11.   1.49   1.418   1.814

12.   0.37   0.312   0.366

13.   8.01   8.108   8.181

14.   21.71   27.1   21.07

15.   2.59   2.81   2.95

16.   7.12   7.22   7.17

17.   0.604   0.641   0.601

Use the place-value chart to order the decimals from least to greatest.

Example

	Ones	Tenths	Hundredths	Thousandths
0.09	0	0	9	0
0.209	0	2	0	9
2.009	2	0	0	9

Compare the ones. Are they the same?　　　Yes / No ___No___

Compare the tenths. Are they the same?　　Yes / No ___No___

___0.09___, ___0.209___, ___2.009___
　least　　　　　　　　　　greatest

18.

	Ones	Tenths	Hundredths	Thousandths
3.586				
0.314				
3.567				

Compare the ones. Are they the same?　　　Yes / No _____

Compare the tenths. Are they the same?　　Yes / No _____

Compare the hundredths. Are they the same?　Yes / No _____

_____, _____, _____
　least　　　　　　　　　　greatest

Order the decimals from least to greatest.

19.   0.103,   0.311,   0.131

20.   5.14,   0.15,   1.44

21.   7.013,   7.131,   7.033

22.   9.090,   9.900,   9.009

23.   0.081,   0.118,   0.180

24.   3.963,   3.936,   3.639

25.   9.449,   4.949,   9.494

26.   6.02,   2.06,   0.62

Use the place-value chart to order the decimals from greatest to least.

Example

	Ones	Tenths	Hundredths	Thousandths
0.426	0	4	2	6
0.5	0	5	0	0
0.19	0	1	9	0

Compare the ones. Are they the same?   Yes / No ___Yes___

Compare the tenths. Are they the same?   Yes / No ___No___

___0.5___, ___0.426___, ___0.19___
greatest   least

27.

	Ones		Tenths	Hundredths	Thousandths
2.396					
1.431					
2.302					

Compare the ones. Are they the same?   Yes / No _____

Compare the tenths. Are they the same?   Yes / No _____

Compare the hundredths. Are they the same?   Yes / No _____

_____, _____, _____

   greatest   least

Order the decimals from greatest to least.

28.   21.12,   12.21,   12.12

29.   0.101,   0.011,   0.110

30.   4.63,   4.36,   4.06

Show the location of each decimal by drawing an X on the number line. Then round the decimal to the nearest hundredth.

31.

   0.14   0.15

0.148 rounded to the nearest hundredth is _____.

32.

4.01   4.02

4.013 rounded to the nearest hundredth is _____.

Round each decimal to the nearest whole number, nearest tenth, and nearest hundredth.

	Decimal	Rounded to the Nearest		
		Whole Number	**Tenth**	**Hundredth**
33.	0.147			
34.	2.564			
35.	6.325			

Fill in the blanks.

36. I am thinking of a decimal. It is 2.77 when rounded to the nearest hundredth. It is smaller than 2.77. What could this decimal be?

_____

37. 1 square meter is equal to 1.195 square yards.
Round 1.195 square yards to the nearest hundredth.

_____

Worksheet 3   Rewriting Decimals as Fractions

Rewrite each decimal as a fraction or mixed number in simplest form.

> **Example**
>
> $0.007 = \dfrac{7}{1000}$

1. $0.8 =$ _____

2. $5.9 =$ _____

3. $6.04 =$ _____

4. $0.47 =$ _____

5. $0.072 =$ _____

6. $7.015 =$ _____

7. $2.436 =$ _____

8. $2.037 =$ _____

9. $4.008 =$ _____

10. $16.15 =$ _____

11. $0.754 =$ _____

12. $0.005 =$ _____

13. $4.36 =$ _____

14.   0.02 = _____

15.   12.06 = _____

16.   11.008 = _____

17.   15.052 = _____

18.   17.814 = _____

19.   19.3 = _____

20.   9.405 = _____

21.   0.108 = _____

22.   4.7 = _____

23.   0.3 = _____

24.   1.345 = _____

25.   0.539 = _____

CHAPTER 9 Multiplying and Dividing Decimals

Worksheet 1   Multiplying Decimals

Multiply. Write the product as a decimal.

Example

2 tenths × 3 = _____6_____ tenths

So, 0.2 × 3 = _____6_____ tenths

= _____0.6_____ .

The **product** is 0.6.

---

1.   4 tenths × 2 = _____ tenths

So, 0.4 × 2 = _____ tenths

= _____ .

2.   3 tenths × 3 = _____ tenths

So, 0.3 × 3 = _____ tenths

= _____ .

3.   8 tenths × 5 = _____ tenths

So, 0.8 × 5 = _____ tenths

= _____ .

4.   4 tenths $\times$ 4 = _____ tenths

So, 0.4 $\times$ 4 = _____ tenths

= _____.

5.   6 tenths $\times$ 7 = _____ tenths

So, 0.6 $\times$ 7 = _____ tenths

= _____.

Multiply.

┌─ *Example* ─────────────────────────────────┐

     0.2 $\times$ 4 = ___*0.8*___

└──┘

6.   0.3 $\times$ 2 = _____

7.   0.3 $\times$ 4 = _____

8.   0.4 $\times$ 6 = _____

Multiply.

┌─ *Example* ─────────────────────────────────┐

$$\begin{array}{r} 0.3 \\ \times \quad 3 \\ \hline 0.9 \end{array}$$

└──┘

9.
$$\begin{array}{r} 0.6 \\ \times \quad 4 \\ \hline \end{array}$$

10.   0.5
         ×   8
         ————

11.   0.7
         ×   3
         ————

12.   0.9
         ×   5
         ————

Fill in the blanks.

13.   4 ones + 20 tenths = _____ ones

14.   6 ones + 30 tenths = _____ ones

15.   9 ones + 40 tenths = _____ ones

16.   24 tenths = _____ ones and _____ tenths

17.   37 tenths = _____ ones and _____ tenths

18.   101 tenths = _____ ones and _____ tenth

Multiply. Fill in the blanks.

Example

4 tenths × 3 = ____12____ tenths

= ____1____ one and ____2____ tenths

19.   6 tenths × 4 = _____ tenths

= _____ ones and _____ tenths

20.   5 tenths × 7 = _____ tenths

= _____ ones and _____ tenths

21.   8 tenths × 6 = _____ tenths

= _____ ones and _____ tenths

Multiply. Fill in the blanks.

Example

2 ones and 4 tenths × 2 = ____4____ ones and ____8____ tenths

22.   3 ones and 2 tenths × 4 = _____ ones and _____ tenths

23.   7 ones and 1 tenth × 6 = _____ ones and _____ tenths

24.   6 ones and 3 tenths × 3 = _____ ones and _____ tenths

Multiply 2.8 by 5. Fill in the blanks.

25. 2.8×5 →   8 tenths $\times$ 5 = _____ tenths

_____ tenths = _____ ones and _____ tenths

2 ones $\times$ 5 = _____ ones

_____ ones + _____ ones = _____ ones

So, $2.8 \times 5 =$ _____.

Multiply 4.7 by 3. Fill in the blanks.

26. 4.7×3 →   7 tenths $\times$ 3 = _____ tenths

_____ tenths = _____ ones and _____ tenth

4 ones $\times$ 3 = _____ ones

_____ ones + _____ ones = _____ ones

So, $4.7 \times 3 =$ _____.

Multiply 5.6 by 4. Fill in the blanks.

27. 5.6×4 →   6 tenths $\times$ 4 = _____ tenths

_____ tenths = _____ ones and _____ tenths

5 ones $\times$ 4 = _____ ones

_____ ones + _____ ones = _____ ones

So, $5.6 \times 4 =$ _____.

Multiply 6.8 by 7. Fill in the blanks.

28.   6.8 × 7 → 8 tenths × 7 = _____ tenths

_____ tenths = _____ ones and _____ tenths

6 ones × 7 = _____ ones

_____ ones + _____ ones = _____ ones

So, 6.8 × 7 = _____.

Multiply 3.7 by 4. Fill in the blanks.

29.   3.7 × 4 → 7 tenths × 4 = _____ tenths

_____ tenths = _____ ones and _____ tenths

3 ones × 4 = _____ ones

_____ ones + _____ ones = _____ ones

So, 3.7 × 4 = _____.

Multiply 1.6 by 6. Fill in the blanks.

30.   1.6 × 6 → 6 tenths × 6 = _____ tenths

_____ tenths = _____ ones and _____ tenths

1 one × 6 = _____ ones

_____ ones + _____ ones = _____ ones

So, 1.6 × 6 = _____.

● **Multiply.**

31.   2.8
       $\times$ 8
       _____

32.   4.7
       $\times$ 7
       _____

33.   6.9
       $\times$ 2
       _____

● **Multiply. Write the product as a decimal.**

> *Example*
>
> 3 hundredths $\times$ 2 = _____6_____ hundredths
>
> So, 0.03 $\times$ 2 = _____6_____ hundredths
>
>   = ___0.06___ .

34.   3 hundredths $\times$ 3 = _____ hundredths

So, 0.03 $\times$ 3 = _____ hundredths

         = _____ .

35.   2 hundredths $\times$ 4 = _____ hundredths

So, 0.02 $\times$ 4 = _____ hundredths

         = _____ .

Multiply. Write the product as a decimal.

36.   0.02 × 3 = _____

37.   0.03 × 4 = _____

38.   0.04 × 4 = _____

39.   0.01 × 5 = _____

Multiply.

40.
$$\begin{array}{r} 0.04 \\ \times\quad 3 \\ \hline \end{array}$$

41.
$$\begin{array}{r} 0.02 \\ \times\quad 9 \\ \hline \end{array}$$

42.
$$\begin{array}{r} 0.05 \\ \times\quad 3 \\ \hline \end{array}$$

43.
$$\begin{array}{r} 0.04 \\ \times\quad 5 \\ \hline \end{array}$$

Fill in the blanks.

> *Example*
>
> 23 hundredths = ____2____ tenths ____3____ hundredths

44.   47 hundredths = _____ tenths _____ hundredths

45.   80 hundredths = _____ tenths _____ hundredths

46.   59 hundredths = _____ tenths _____ hundredths

Fill in the blanks.

47. 4 hundredths + 8 hundredths = _____ hundredths

= _____ tenth _____ hundredths

48. 9 hundredths + 5 hundredths = _____ hundredths

= _____ tenth _____ hundredths

Multiply. Fill in the blanks.

> *Example*
>
> 5 hundredths × 3 = ___15___ hundredths
>
> = ___1___ tenth ___5___ hundredths

49. 4 hundredths × 7 = _____ hundredths

= _____ tenths _____ hundredths

50. 6 hundredths × 8 = _____ hundredths

= _____ tenths _____ hundredths

Multiply. Fill in the blanks.

> *Example*
>
> 4 tenths 2 hundredths × 2 = ___8___ tenths +
>
> ___0___ tenths ___4___ hundredths
>
> = ___8___ tenths ___4___ hundredths

51. 1 tenth 4 hundredths × 6 = _____ tenths +

_____ tenths _____ hundredths

= _____ tenths _____ hundredths

52. 2 tenths 3 hundredths × 7 = _____ tenths +

_____ tenths _____ hundredth

= _____ tenths _____ hundredth

53. 3 tenths 2 hundredths × 8 = _____ tenths +

_____ tenth _____ hundredths

= _____ tenths _____ hundredths

Multiply 0.08 by 3. Fill in the blanks.

54. 8 hundredths × 3 = _____ hundredths

= _____ tenths _____ hundredths

So, 0.08 × 3 = _____.

Multiply 0.05 by 7. Fill in the blanks.

55. 5 hundredths × 7 = _____ hundredths

= _____ tenths _____ hundredths

So, 0.05 × 7 = _____.

Multiply 0.49 by 2. Fill in the blanks.

56.   9 hundredths $\times$ 2 = _____ hundredths

_____ hundredths = _____ tenth _____ hundredths

4 tenths $\times$ 2 = _____ tenths

_____ tenth + _____ tenths = _____ tenths

_____ tenths = _____ ones and _____ tenths

So, 0.49 $\times$ 2 = _____.

Multiply 0.25 by 3. Fill in the blanks.

57.   5 hundredths $\times$ 3 = _____ hundredths

_____ hundredths = _____ tenth _____ hundredths

2 tenths $\times$ 3 = _____ tenths

_____ tenth + _____ tenths = _____ tenths

_____ tenths = _____ ones and _____ tenths

So, 0.25 $\times$ 3 = _____.

Multiply 0.43 by 4. Fill in the blanks.

58.   3 hundredths $\times$ 4 = _____ hundredths

_____ hundredths = _____ tenth _____ hundredths

4 tenths $\times$ 4 = _____ tenths

_____ tenth + _____ tenths = _____ tenths

_____ tenths = _____ one and _____ tenths

So, 0.43 $\times$ 4 = _____.

Multiply 0.67 by 5. Fill in the blanks.

59. 7 hundredths $\times$ 5 = _____ hundredths

_____ hundredths = _____ tenths _____ hundredths

6 tenths $\times$ 5 = _____ tenths

_____ tenths + _____ tenths = _____ tenths

_____ tenths = _____ ones and _____ tenths

So, 0.67 $\times$ 5 = _____.

Multiply.

60.
$$
\begin{array}{r}
1.45 \\
\times \quad 3 \\
\hline
\end{array}
$$

61.
$$
\begin{array}{r}
2.36 \\
\times \quad 4 \\
\hline
\end{array}
$$

62.
$$
\begin{array}{r}
3.58 \\
\times \quad 6 \\
\hline
\end{array}
$$

Worksheet 2   Multiplying by Tens, Hundreds, and Thousands

Place the decimal point in the correct place in the product.

Example

4.35 × 10 = 4 3 . 5

When you multiply a decimal by 10, move the decimal point 1 decimal place to the right.

---

1.   1.28 × 10 = 1 2 8

2.   4.75 × 10 = 4 7 5

3.   0.36 × 10 = 3 6

4.   0.92 × 10 = 9 2

5.   3.45 × 10 = 3 4 5

6.   0.81 × 10 = 8 1

7.   6.4 × 10 = 6 4

8.   7.8 × 10 = 7 8

9.   0.7 × 10 = 7

10.   0.9 × 10 = 9

11.   5.3 × 10 = 5 3

12.   0.4 × 10 = 4

13.   0.375 × 10 = 3 7 5

14.   0.284 × 10 = 2 8 4

15.   1.693 × 10 = 1 6 9 3

16.   2.438 × 10 = 2 4 3 8

17.   0.736 × 10 = 7 3 6

18.   8.931 × 10 = 8 9 3 1

Multiply.

19. $1.39 \times 10 =$ _____

20. $2.47 \times 10 =$ _____

21. $0.84 \times 10 =$ _____

22. $0.94 \times 10 =$ _____

23. $7.2 \times 10 =$ _____

24. $6.3 \times 10 =$ _____

25. $0.8 \times 10 =$ _____

26. $0.2 \times 10 =$ _____

27. $0.481 \times 10 =$ _____

28. $0.179 \times 10 =$ _____

29. $2.435 \times 10 =$ _____

30. $6.582 \times 10 =$ _____

Complete.

31. $0.478 \times$ _____ $= 4.78$

32. $0.07 \times$ _____ $= 0.7$

33. $0.59 \times$ _____ $= 5.9$

34. $0.26 \times$ _____ $= 2.6$

35. _____ $\times 10 = 12.08$

36. _____ $\times 10 = 1.03$

37. _____ $\times 10 = 3.05$

38. _____ $\times 10 = 245.8$

39. $40 =$ _____ $\times 10$

40. $70 = 7 \times$ _____

41. $150 =$ _____ $\times 10$

42. $120 = 12 \times$ _____

43. $8 \times$ _____ $= 80$

44. _____ $\times 10 = 90$

45. $16 \times$ _____ $= 160$

46. _____ $\times 10 = 170$

Complete.

> **Example**
>
> $5 \times 40 = 5 \times \underline{\quad 4 \quad} \times 10$
>
> $\qquad = \underline{\quad 20 \quad} \times 10$
>
> $\qquad = \underline{\quad 200 \quad}$

47. $6 \times 70 = 6 \times \underline{\qquad} \times 10$

$\qquad = \underline{\qquad} \times 10$

$\qquad = \underline{\qquad}$

48. $8 \times 120 = \underline{\qquad} \times \underline{\qquad} \times 10$

$\qquad = \underline{\qquad} \times 10$

$\qquad = \underline{\qquad}$

49. $11 \times 50 = \underline{\qquad} \times \underline{\qquad} \times 10$

$\qquad = \underline{\qquad} \times 10$

$\qquad = \underline{\qquad}$

50. $16 \times 180 = \underline{\qquad} \times \underline{\qquad} \times 10$

$\qquad = \underline{\qquad} \times 10$

$\qquad = \underline{\qquad}$

Find each product.

> *Example*
>
> $6 \times 80 =$ _____480_____
>
>
>
> $6 \times 8 = 48$
> $6 \times 80 = 480$

51. $7 \times 90 =$ _____

52. $9 \times 50 =$ _____

53. $12 \times 40 =$ _____

54. $13 \times 60 =$ _____

55. $15 \times 50 =$ _____

56. $18 \times 30 =$ _____

Place the decimal point in the correct place in the product.

> *Example*
>
> $2.54 \times 100 = 2\ 5\ 4.$
>
>
>
> When you multiply a decimal by 100, move the decimal point 2 decimal places to the right.

57. $1.375 \times 100 = 1\ 3\ 7\ 5$

58.   2.679 × 100 = 2 6 7 9

59.   0.472 × 100 = 4 7 2

60.   0.814 × 100 = 8 1 4

61.   5.78 × 100 = 5 7 8

62.   6.93 × 100 = 6 9 3

63.   0.38 × 100 = 3 8

64.   0.91 × 100 = 9 1

Place the decimal point in the correct place in the product.

> *Example*
>
> 0.213 × 1,000 = 2 1 3.
>
> When you multiply a decimal by 1,000, move the decimal point 3 decimal places to the right.

65.   1.492 × 1,000 = 1 4 9 2

66.   2.679 × 1,000 = 2 6 7 9

67.   0.385 × 1,000 = 3 8 5

68.   0.496 × 1,000 = 4 9 6

69.   4.67 × 1,000 = 4 6 7

70. $5.82 \times 1,000 = 5\ 8\ 2$

71. $0.4 \times 1,000 = 4$

72. $0.1 \times 1,000 = 1$

Complete.

73. $0.583 \times$ _____ $= 58.3$ **74.** $0.07 \times$ _____ $= 70$

75. $0.481 \times$ _____ $= 48.1$ **76.** $0.032 \times$ _____ $= 32$

77. _____ $\times 100 = 36.9$ **78.** _____ $\times 1,000 = 204$

79. _____ $\times 1,000 = 48$ **80.** _____ $\times 100 = 91$

81. $500 =$ _____ $\times 100$ **82.** $8,000 = 8 \times$ _____

83. $9,000 =$ _____ $\times 1,000$ **84.** $1,400 = 14 \times$ _____

85. $7 \times$ _____ $= 700$ **86.** _____ $\times 1,000 = 6,000$

87. $13 \times$ _____ $= 13,000$ **88.** _____ $\times 100 = 2,600$

Complete.

> *Example*
>
> $4 \times 500 = 4 \times \underline{\quad 5 \quad} \times 100$
>
> $\qquad\qquad = \underline{\quad 20 \quad} \times 100$
>
> $\qquad\qquad = \underline{\quad 2,000 \quad}$

89. $3 \times 8{,}000 = 3 \times \underline{\hspace{2cm}} \times 1{,}000$

$= \underline{\hspace{2cm}} \times 1{,}000$

$= \underline{\hspace{2cm}}$

90. $7 \times 1{,}100 = \underline{\hspace{2cm}} \times \underline{\hspace{2cm}} \times 100$

$= \underline{\hspace{2cm}} \times 100$

$= \underline{\hspace{2cm}}$

91. $12 \times 6{,}000 = \underline{\hspace{2cm}} \times \underline{\hspace{2cm}} \times 1{,}000$

$= \underline{\hspace{2cm}} \times 1{,}000$

$= \underline{\hspace{2cm}}$

Find each product.

> *Example*
>
> $7 \times 400 = \underline{\ 2{,}800\ }$
>
> $7 \times 4 = 28$
> $7 \times 400 = 2{,}800$

92. $4 \times 8{,}000 = \underline{\hspace{2cm}}$

93. $6 \times 900 = \underline{\hspace{2cm}}$

94. $5 \times 6{,}000 = \underline{\hspace{2cm}}$

95. $8 \times 700 = \underline{\hspace{2cm}}$

Find each product.

> *Example*
>
> $0.37 \times 200 = $ _____74_____
>
> $0.37 \times 2 = 0.74$
> $0.37 \times 200 = 74$
>
>

96. $0.13 \times 700 = $ _____

97. $1.2 \times 8{,}000 = $ _____

98. $1.5 \times 600 = $ _____

99. $0.17 \times 4{,}000 = $ _____

Worksheet 3   Dividing Decimals

Divide. Fill in the blanks.

1.   9 tenths ÷ 3 = _____ tenths

2.   8 tenths ÷ 2 = _____ tenths

3.   6 hundredths ÷ 2 = _____ hundredths

4.   12 hundredths ÷ 4 = _____ hundredths

5.   25 hundredths ÷ 5 = _____ hundredths

6.   16 tenths ÷ 4 = _____ tenths

7.   28 hundredths ÷ 7 = _____ hundredths

8.   48 hundredths ÷ 6 = _____ hundredths

9.   64 hundredths ÷ 8 = _____ hundredths

10.   92 hundredths ÷ 4 = _____ hundredths

11.   15 tenths ÷ 3 = _____ tenths

12.   24 tenths ÷ 6 = _____ tenths

13.   56 hundredths ÷ 8 = _____ hundredths

14.   70 hundredths ÷ 5 = _____ hundredths

15.   81 hundredths ÷ 9 = _____ hundredths

Divide 0.42 by 6. Fill in the blanks.

Example

The **quotient** is 0.07.

Divide 4.6 by 2. Fill in the blanks.

16.

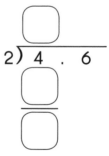

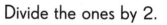

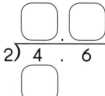

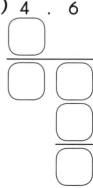

Divide the ones by 2.

4 ones ÷ 2 = _____ ones

Divide the tenths by 2.

6 tenths ÷ 2 = _____ tenths

So, 4.6 ÷ 2 = _____.

Divide 6.9 by 3. Fill in the blanks.

17.

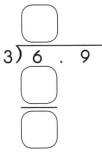

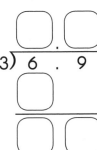

Divide the ones by 3.

6 ones ÷ 3 = _____ ones

Divide the tenths by 3.

9 tenths ÷ 3 = _____ tenths

So, 6.9 ÷ 3 = _____.

Divide 8.4 by 4. Fill in the blanks.

18.

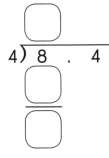

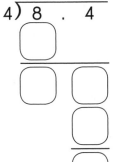

Divide the ones by 4.

8 ones ÷ 4 = _____ ones

Divide the tenths by 4.

4 tenths ÷ 4 = _____ tenth

So, 8.4 ÷ 4 = _____.

Divide.

19.

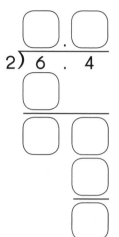

20.

21.

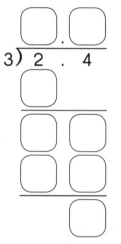

22.

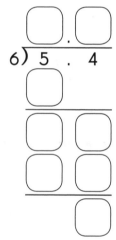

23.

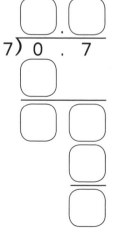

24.

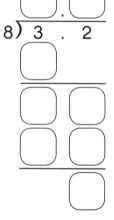

Regroup. Then divide.

25.   4.29 ÷ 3

4 ones = _____ ones and 10 tenths

4 ones and 2 tenths = 3 ones and 10 tenths + 2 tenths

= 3 ones and _____ tenths

3 ones and _____ tenths 9 hundredths ÷ 3

= _____ one and _____ tenths _____ hundredths

26.   3.68 ÷ 2

3 ones = _____ ones and 10 tenths

3 ones and 6 tenths = _____ ones and 10 tenths + _____ tenths

= _____ ones and _____ tenths

2 ones and _____ tenths _____ hundredths ÷ 2

= _____ one and _____ tenths _____ hundredths

27.   6.54 ÷ 3

5 tenths = _____ tenths 20 hundredths

5 tenths 4 hundredths

= _____ tenths 20 hundredths + _____ hundredths

= _____ tenths _____ hundredths

6 ones and _____ tenths _____ hundredths ÷ 3

= _____ ones and _____ tenth _____ hundredths

28. 4.64 ÷ 4

6 tenths = _____ tenths _____ hundredths

6 tenths 4 hundredths

= _____ tenths _____ hundredths + _____ hundredths

= _____ tenths _____ hundredths

4 ones and _____ tenths _____ hundredths ÷ 4

= _____ one and _____ tenth _____ hundredths

29. 4.95 ÷ 3

4 ones = _____ ones and _____ tenths

9 tenths 5 hundredths

= _____ tenths _____ hundredths + _____ hundredths

= _____ tenths _____ hundredths

3 ones and _____ tenths _____ hundredths ÷ 3

= _____ one and _____ tenths _____ hundredths

30. 6.55 ÷ 5

6 ones = _____ ones and _____ tenths

6 ones and 5 tenths = _____ ones and _____ tenths + _____ tenths

= _____ ones and _____ tenths

5 ones and _____ tenths _____ hundredths ÷ 5

= _____ one and _____ tenths _____ hundredth

Divide 4.56 by 2. Fill in the blanks.

31.

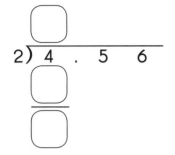

$$2) \overline{4 \,.\, 5 \quad 6}$$

Divide the ones by 2.

4 ones ÷ 2 = _____ ones

$$2) \overline{4 \,.\, 5 \quad 6}$$

Divide the tenths by 2.

5 tenths ÷ 2 = _____ tenths R _____ tenth

_____ tenth = _____ hundredths

$$2) \overline{4 \,.\, 5 \quad 6}$$

Add the hundredths.

_____ hundredths + _____ hundredths

= _____ hundredths

Divide the hundredths by 2.

_____ hundredths ÷ 2

= _____ hundredths

So, 4.56 ÷ 2 = _____.

Divide 6.57 by 3. Fill in the blanks.

32.

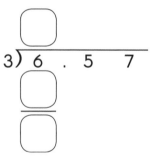

Divide the ones by 3.

6 ones ÷ 3 = _____ ones

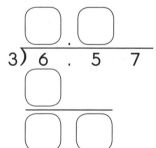

Divide the tenths by 3.

5 tenths ÷ 3 = _____ tenth R _____ tenths

_____ tenths = _____ hundredths

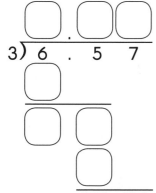

Add the hundredths.

_____ hundredths + _____ hundredths

= _____ hundredths

Divide the hundredths by 3.

_____ hundredths ÷ 3

= _____ hundredths

So, 6.57 ÷ 3 = _____.

Divide.

33.

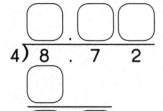
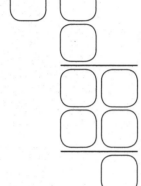

34.

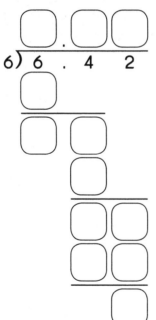

Divide 5.48 by 2. Fill in the blanks.

35.

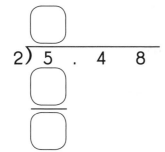

Divide the ones by 2.

5 ones ÷ 2 = _____ ones R _____ one

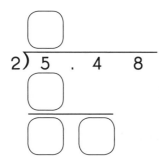

Regroup the remainder _____ one.

_____ one = _____ tenths

Add the tenths.

_____ tenths + _____ tenths = _____ tenths

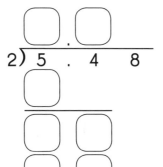

Divide the tenths by 2.

_____ tenths ÷ 2 = _____ tenths

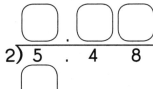
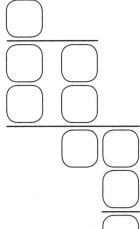

Divide the hundredths by 2.

_____ hundredths ÷ 2

= _____ hundredths

So, 5.48 ÷ 2 = _____.

Divide 6.78 by 3. Fill in the blanks.

36.

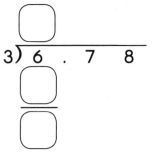

Divide the ones by 3.

6 ones ÷ 3 = _____ ones

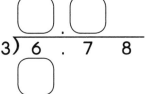
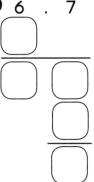

Divide the tenths by 3.

_____ tenths ÷ 3 = _____ tenths R _____ tenth

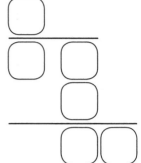

Regroup the remainder ____ tenth.

____ tenth = ____ hundredths

Add the hundredths.

____ hundredths + ____ hundredths

= ____ hundredths

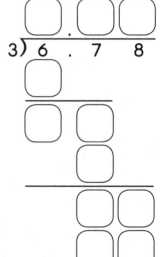

Divide the hundredths by 3.

____ hundredths ÷ 3

= ____ hundredths

So, $6.78 \div 3 =$ _____.

Divide.

37.

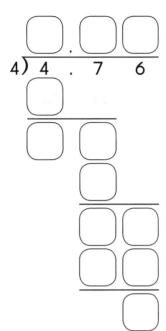

38.

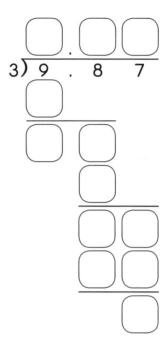

39.

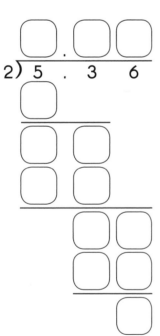

40.

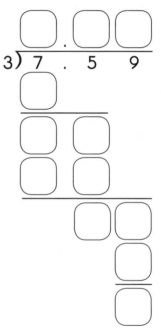

41.

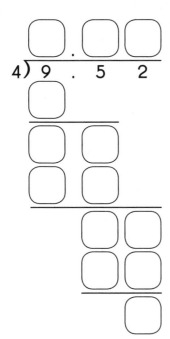

42.

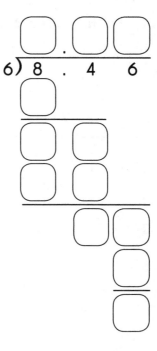

Divide.

43. $0.48 \div 2 =$ _____

44. $0.36 \div 2 =$ _____

45. $4.56 \div 2 =$ _____

46. $1.58 \div 2 =$ _____

47. $3.76 \div 2 =$ _____

48. $0.96 \div 3 =$ _____

49. $0.54 \div 3 =$ _____

50. $6.93 \div 3 =$ _____

51. $4.71 \div 3 =$ _____

52. $5.28 \div 3 =$ _____

53. $0.56 \div 4 =$ _____

54. $0.75 \div 5 =$ _____

55. $5.82 \div 6 =$ _____

56. $8.61 \div 7 =$ _____

57. $5.28 \div 8 =$ _____

Name: _____   Date: _____

Divide. Round each quotient to the nearest tenth.

Example

```
    1 . 6  6
3) 5 . 0  0
   3
   2  0
   1  8
      2  0
      1  8
         2
```

$5 \div 3$ is about 1.7.

58.

$2 \div 3$ is about _____.

59.

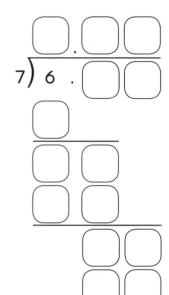

$6 \div 7$ is about _____.

60.

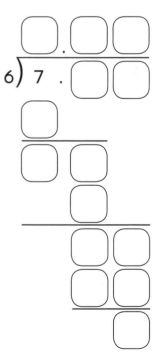

$7 \div 6$ is about _____.

Divide. Round each quotient to the nearest hundredth.

61.   5 ÷ 9

62.   8 ÷ 7

63.   11 ÷ 3

Worksheet 4 Dividing by Tens, Hundreds, and Thousands

Place the decimal point in the correct place in the quotient.

> *Example*
>
> $7.26 \div 10 = 0.726$
>
> When you divide a number by 10, move the decimal point 1 decimal place to the left.

1. $1.37 \div 10 =$ 1 3 7

2. $3.85 \div 10 =$ 3 8 5

3. $36.2 \div 10 =$ 3 6 2

4. $94.7 \div 10 =$ 9 4 7

5. $645 \div 10 =$ 6 4 5

6. $786 \div 10 =$ 7 8 6

7. $0.9 \div 10 =$ 9

8. $0.4 \div 10 =$ 4

Complete.

9. $2.84 \div 10 =$ _____

10. $463 \div 10 =$ _____

11. $0.95 \div 10 =$ _____

12. $72.6 \div 10 =$ _____

Complete.

13. $57.8 \div$ _____ $= 5.78$

14. $4 \div$ _____ $= 0.4$

15. $894 \div$ _____ $= 89.4$

16. $0.26 \div$ _____ $= 0.026$

17. _____ $\div 10 = 3.09$

18. _____ $\div 10 = 70.4$

19. _____ $\div 10 = 0.05$

20. _____ $\div 10 = 0.458$

Complete.

21. $90 \div 30 = (90 \div \underline{\hspace{2cm}}) \div 10$

22. $140 \div 20 = (140 \div \underline{\hspace{2cm}}) \div 10$

23. $280 \div 40 = (\underline{\hspace{2cm}} \div 4) \div 10$

24. $420 \div 70 = (\underline{\hspace{2cm}} \div 7) \div 10$

Complete.

25. $60 \div 20 = (60 \div \underline{\hspace{2cm}}) \div 10$

$= \underline{\hspace{2cm}} \div 10$

$= \underline{\hspace{2cm}}$

26. $120 \div 30 = (120 \div \underline{\hspace{2cm}}) \div 10$

$= \underline{\hspace{2cm}} \div 10$

$= \underline{\hspace{2cm}}$

27. $360 \div 40 = (\underline{\hspace{2cm}} \div 4) \div 10$

$= \underline{\hspace{2cm}} \div 10$

$= \underline{\hspace{2cm}}$

28. $560 \div 80 = (\underline{\hspace{2cm}} \div 8) \div 10$

$= \underline{\hspace{2cm}} \div 10$

$= \underline{\hspace{2cm}}$

29. $16 \div 80 = ($ _____ $\div 8) \div 10$

   $= $ _____ $\div 10$

   $= $ _____

30. $21 \div 70 = ($ _____ $\div 7) \div 10$

   $= $ _____ $\div 10$

   $= $ _____

31. $0.9 \div 30 = ($ _____ $\div 3) \div 10$

   $= $ _____ $\div 10$

   $= $ _____

32. $0.15 \div 50 = ($ _____ $\div 5) \div 10$

   $= $ _____ $\div 10$

   $= $ _____

Divide.

33. $1.4 \div 70 = $ _____

34. $8 \div 40 = $ _____

35. $9 \div 30 = $ _____

36. $0.75 \div 50 = $ _____

37. $0.42 \div 70 = $ _____

Place the decimal point in the correct place in the quotient.

> **Example**
>
> $61.5 \div 100 = 0.6\ 1\ 5$
>
> When you divide a number by 100, move the decimal point 2 decimal places to the left.

38. $23.8 \div 100 = \quad 2\ 3\ 8$ **39.** $47.3 \div 100 = \quad 4\ 7\ 3$

40. $37.5 \div 100 = \quad 3\ 7\ 5$ **41.** $98.4 \div 100 = \quad 9\ 8\ 4$

42. $5.9 \div 100 = \quad 5\ 9$ **43.** $2.7 \div 100 = \quad 2\ 7$

Place the decimal point in the correct place in the quotient.

> **Example**
>
> $715 \div 1,000 = 0.7\ 1\ 5$
>
> When you divide a number by 1,000, move the decimal point 3 decimal places to the left.

44. $147 \div 1,000 = \quad 1\ 4\ 7$ **45.** $258 \div 1,000 = \quad 2\ 5\ 8$

46. $69 \div 1,000 = \quad 6\ 9$ **47.** $38 \div 1,000 = \quad 3\ 8$

48. $1,234 \div 1,000 = \quad 1\ 2\ 3\ 4$ **49.** $6,101 \div 1,000 = \quad 6\ 1\ 0\ 1$

Name: _____   **Date:** _____

Complete.

50. $36.9 \div$ _____ $= 0.369$ **51.** $4 \div$ _____ $= 0.004$

52. $78 \div$ _____ $= 0.078$ **53.** $49.6 \div$ _____ $= 0.496$

54. _____ $\div 100 = 4.08$ **55.** _____ $\div 100 = 2.05$

56. _____ $\div 1{,}000 = 0.007$ **57.** _____ $\div 1{,}000 = 0.852$

Complete.

58. $800 \div 200 = (800 \div$ _____$) \div 100$

59. $1{,}500 \div 300 = (1{,}500 \div$ _____$) \div 100$

60. $40 \div 800 = ($_____ $\div 8) \div 100$

61. $6 \div 200 = ($_____ $\div 2) \div 100$

62. $0.9 \div 300 = ($_____ $\div 3) \div 100$

63. $600 \div 2{,}000 = (600 \div$ _____$) \div 1{,}000$

64. $1{,}800 \div 3{,}000 = (1{,}800 \div$ _____$) \div 1{,}000$

65. $180 \div 9{,}000 = ($_____ $\div 9) \div 1{,}000$

66. $8 \div 2{,}000 = ($_____ $\div 2) \div 1{,}000$

67. $0.8 \div 4{,}000 = ($_____ $\div 4) \div 1{,}000$

Complete.

68. $40 \div 200 = $ _____

69. $60 \div 3{,}000 = $ _____

70. $320 \div 800 = $ _____

71. $810 \div 9{,}000 = $ _____

72. $12 \div 3{,}000 = $ _____

73. $25 \div 5{,}000 = $ _____

74. $5 \div 100 = $ _____

75. $8 \div 400 = $ _____

76. $0.4 \div 200 = $ _____

77. $9 \div 600 = $ _____

78. $6 \div 2{,}000 = $ _____

79. $40 \div 5{,}000 = $ _____

80. $70 \div 1{,}000 = $ _____

81. $600 \div 4{,}000 = $ _____

82. $1{,}400 \div 500 = $ _____

83. $7{,}500 \div 1{,}500 = $ _____

Worksheet 5   Estimating Decimals

Round each decimal to the nearest whole number. Fill in the blanks.

Example

1.375 is about ___1___.   3 tenths is ___less than___ ___5___ tenths.

1.375 → 1

1.   12.459 is about _____.   4 tenths is _____ _____ tenths.

12.459 → _____

2.   43.607 is about _____.   6 tenths is _____ _____ tenths.

43.607 → _____

3.   28.910 is about _____.   9 tenths is _____ _____ tenths.

28.910 → _____

Round each number to the nearest tenth. Fill in the blanks.

Example

2.483 is about ___2.5___.   8 hundredths is ___greater than___ ___5___ hundredths.

2.483 → ___2.5___

4.   6.341 is about _____.   4 hundredths is _____ _____ hundredths.

6.341 → _____

5.   17.251 is about _____.   5 hundredths is _____ _____ hundredths.

17.251 → _____

6. 39.908 is about _____. 0 hundredths is _____ _____ hundredths.

$$39.908 \longrightarrow \text{_____}$$

7. 18.472 is about _____. 7 hundredths is _____ _____ hundredths.

$$18.472 \longrightarrow \text{_____}$$

Round each number to the nearest hundredth. Fill in the blanks.

> *Example*
>
> 1.284 is about _1.28_. 4 thousandths is _less than_ _5_ thousandths.
>
> $$1.284 \longrightarrow \underline{1.28}$$

8. 16.016 is about _____. 6 thousandths is _____ _____ thousandths.

$$16.016 \longrightarrow \text{_____}$$

9. 24.005 is about _____. 5 thousandths _____ _____ thousandths.

$$24.005 \longrightarrow \text{_____}$$

10. 45.076 is about _____. 6 thousandths is _____ _____ thousandths.

$$45.076 \longrightarrow \text{_____}$$

Round each decimal to the nearest whole number. Then estimate the sum.

> *Example*
>
> 0.47 + 2.52 is about _3_. 0.47 $\longrightarrow$ _0_; 2.52 $\longrightarrow$ _3_
>
> $$0 + 3 = \underline{3}$$

11. 1.62 + 3.39 is about _____. 1.62 $\longrightarrow$ _____; 3.39 $\longrightarrow$ _____

$$\text{_____} + \text{_____} = \text{_____}$$

12. 4.53 + 0.82 is about _____. 4.53 ⟶ _____; 0.82 ⟶ _____

_____ + _____ = _____

13. 7.49 + 2.39 is about _____. 7.49 ⟶ _____; 2.39 ⟶ _____

_____ + _____ = _____

14. 18.57 + 9.98 is about _____. 18.57 ⟶ _____; 9.98 ⟶ _____

_____ + _____ = _____

15. 4.67 + 0.88 is about _____. 4.67 ⟶ _____; 0.88 ⟶ _____

_____ + _____ = _____

Round each number to the nearest tenth. Then estimate the sum or difference.

> *Example*
>
> 0.51 + 2.48 is about ___3___. 0.51 ⟶ ___0.5___; 2.48 ⟶ ___2.5___
>
> ___0.5___ + ___2.5___ = ___3___

16. 7.39 − 2.91 is about _____. 7.39 ⟶ _____; 2.91 ⟶ _____

_____ − _____ = _____

17. 0.87 + 1.49 is about _____.

18. 12.39 − 4.72 is about _____.

19.   18.59 − 9.66 is about _____.

20.   21.85 + 0.75 is about _____.

Round each decimal to the nearest whole number. Then estimate the product.

Example

2.47 × 4 is about ____8____.   2.47 → ____2____

____2____ × 4 = ____8____

---

21.   3.51 × 7 is about _____.   3.51 → _____

_____ × _____ = _____

22.   12.07 × 8 is about _____.

23.   15.76 × 11 is about _____.

24.   18.32 × 12 is about _____.

25.   27.13 × 13 is about _____.

Round each decimal to the nearest tenth. Then estimate the product.

> *Example*
>
> 3.45 × 4 is about ___14___. 3.45 ⟶ 3.5
>
> ___3.5___ × 4 = ___14___

26. 4.54 × 6 is about _____. 4.54 ⟶ _____

_____ × _____ = _____

27. 14.27 × 7 is about _____.

28. 16.94 × 9 is about _____.

Round each decimal to the nearest whole number. Then estimate the quotient.

> *Example*
>
> 12.49 ÷ 4 is about ___3___. 12.49 ⟶ ___12___
>
> ___12___ ÷ 4 = ___3___

29. 31.52 ÷ 8 is about _____. 31.52 ⟶ _____

_____ ÷ _____ = _____

30. 71.63 ÷ 9 is about _____.

31. 62.55 ÷ 7 is about _____.

Estimate. Round the decimals to the nearest tenth.

> *Example*
>
> 12.77 ÷ 4 is about ___3.2___.   12.77 ⟶ ___12.8___
>
> ___12.8___ ÷ 4 = ___3.2___

32.   37.24 ÷ 6 is about _____.   37.24 ⟶ _____

_____ ÷ _____ = _____

33.   21.64 ÷ 8 is about _____.

34.   51.09 ÷ 7 is about _____.

Worksheet 6 Real-World Problems: Decimals

Solve. Show you work.

1. The length of a biscuit is 3.2 centimeters. John places four biscuits side by side in a row. Estimate the total length of the row of biscuits.

    3.2 cm ⟶ _____ cm

    _____ × _____ = _____ cm

    The total length is about _____ centimeters.

2. Rose joins 6 pieces of ribbon. Each piece of ribbon is 7.57 centimeters long. Estimate the total length of the 6 pieces of ribbon.

    The total length is about _____ centimeters.

3. Kim has $78.65. She distributes her money equally among her 6 children. Estimate the amount of money each child gets.

78.65 ⟶ 6 × _____ = _____   6 × _____ = _____

    6 × _____ = _____

_____ is nearer to 78.

Since 6 × _____ = 78, each child gets about $_____.

4. Brad has a rope that is 65 meters long. He wants to cut the rope into 4 equal parts. Find the length of each cut part to the nearest meter.

Hint: Think of a number that when multiplied by 4 is close to 65.

65 ⟶ 4 × _____ = _____   4 × _____ = _____

    4 × _____ = _____

_____ is nearer to 65.

Since 4 × _____ = _____, the length of each cut part of the rope is

about _____ meters.

5. Jennifer has $20 with her. She wants to buy the following items to bake a cake: a bag of flour for $6.80, a tray of eggs for $4.50, and a bag of sugar for $7.75. Does Jennifer have enough money to buy all three items?

6. The capacity of a pail is 2.17 liters. Yumiko fills 9 of these pails with water in order to fill a larger bucket. Find the capacity of the larger bucket. Round your answer to the nearest liter.

7. Tommy drove 15.67 miles from home to Paddle Middle School to get his brother Johnny. They stopped for a lemonade at a café that is 8.92 miles from home. What is the distance between the café and the school? Give your answer to the nearest mile.

8. Shane is training for the National Vertical Marathon. His best time so far is 9.33 minutes. Shane wants to complete the marathon in 7.5 minutes. How much time must Shane shave off his best time to achieve his goal? Give your answer to the nearest minute.

A vertical marathon is a competition where one has to try to run up many flights of stairs (usually in a tall building) and complete it in as short a time as possible.

CHAPTER 10 Percent

Worksheet 1   Percent

Each 10 × 10 grid has some shaded parts. Fill in the blanks to describe each grid.

Example

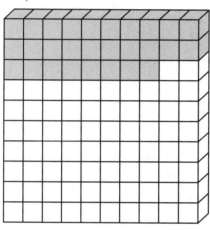

_____28_____ out of 100 parts are shaded.

_____28_____% of the whole is shaded.

_____72_____ out of 100 parts are **not** shaded.

_____72_____% of the whole is **not** shaded.

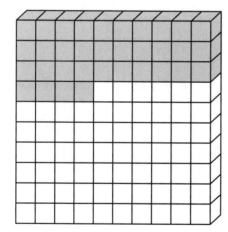

1. _____ out of 100 parts are shaded.

2. _____% of the whole is shaded.

3. _____ out of 100 parts are **not** shaded.

4. _____% of the whole is **not** shaded.

Express each fraction as a percent.

> *Example*
>
> $\dfrac{74}{100} = \underline{\quad 74 \quad}\%$

5. $\dfrac{18}{100} = \underline{\hspace{2cm}}\%$

6. $\dfrac{55}{100} = \underline{\hspace{2cm}}\%$

7. $\dfrac{63}{100} = \underline{\hspace{2cm}}\%$

Express each fraction as a percent.

> *Example*
>
> $\dfrac{3}{10} = \dfrac{\boxed{30}}{100}$
>
> $\phantom{\dfrac{3}{10}} = \underline{\quad 30 \quad}\%$

8. $\dfrac{9}{10} = \dfrac{\boxed{}}{100}$

$\phantom{\dfrac{9}{10}} = \underline{\hspace{2cm}}\%$

9. $\dfrac{7}{10} = \dfrac{\boxed{}}{100}$

$\phantom{\dfrac{7}{10}} = \underline{\hspace{2cm}}\%$

10. $\dfrac{8}{10} = \dfrac{\boxed{}}{100}$

$\phantom{\dfrac{8}{10}} = \underline{\hspace{2cm}}\%$

Express each decimal as a percent.

Example

$$0.24 = \dfrac{\boxed{24}}{100}$$

$$= \underline{\quad 24 \quad}\%$$

11. $0.4 = \dfrac{\boxed{}}{100}$

$= \underline{\hspace{2cm}}\%$

12. $0.79 = \dfrac{\boxed{}}{100}$

$= \underline{\hspace{2cm}}\%$

13. $0.46 = \dfrac{\boxed{}}{100}$

$= \underline{\hspace{2cm}}\%$

14. $0.01 = \dfrac{\boxed{}}{100}$

$= \underline{\hspace{2cm}}\%$

15. $0.08 = \dfrac{\boxed{}}{100}$

$= \underline{\hspace{2cm}}\%$

16. $0.09 = \dfrac{\boxed{}}{100}$

$= \underline{\hspace{2cm}}\%$

Express each percent as a fraction.

> **Example**
>
> $27\% = \dfrac{\boxed{27}}{\boxed{100}}$

17. $21\% = \dfrac{\square}{\square}$

18. $63\% = \dfrac{\square}{\square}$

19. $9\% = \dfrac{\square}{\square}$

20. $3\% = \dfrac{\square}{\square}$

Express each percent as a decimal.

> **Example**
>
> $18\% = \dfrac{\boxed{18}}{100} = \underline{\quad 0.18 \quad}$

21. $37\% = \dfrac{\square}{100} = \underline{\qquad}$

22. $94\% = \dfrac{\square}{100} = \underline{\qquad}$

23. $5\% = \dfrac{\square}{100} = \underline{\qquad}$

24. $9\% = \dfrac{\square}{100} = \underline{\qquad}$

Express each fraction in simplest form.

25. $\dfrac{36}{100} = \dfrac{\boxed{}}{\boxed{}}$

26. $\dfrac{15}{100} = \dfrac{\boxed{}}{\boxed{}}$

27. $\dfrac{72}{100} = \dfrac{\boxed{}}{\boxed{}}$

28. $\dfrac{18}{100} = \dfrac{\boxed{}}{\boxed{}}$

Express each percent as a fraction in simplest form.

> **Example**
>
> $20\% = \dfrac{\boxed{20}}{100}$
>
> $ = \underline{\ \dfrac{1}{5}\ }$

29. $42\% = \dfrac{\boxed{}}{100}$

$ = \underline{}$

30. $75\% = \dfrac{\boxed{}}{100}$

$ = \underline{}$

31. $8\% = \dfrac{\boxed{}}{100}$

$ = \underline{}$

32. $5\% = \dfrac{\boxed{}}{100}$

   $= \underline{\hspace{3cm}}$

Express each item as a percent, and then as a decimal.

		Percent	**Decimal**
33.	7 out of 100		
34.	4 out of 10		
35.	9 out of 10		

Express each item as a decimal, and then as a fraction.

		Decimal	**Fraction**
36.	0%		
37.	8%		
38.	33%		
39.	74%		
40.	100%		

Express each item as a percent, and then as a fraction.

		Percent	Fraction
41.	0		
42.	0.7		
43.	0.44		
44.	0.73		
45.	1		

Fill in the blanks.

46. Samantha had $100. She spent $45 on a meal.

Money spent = _____%

Money left = _____%

47. A tank contained 10 liters of water. Alvin poured out some water from the tank and there were 3 liters of water left.

Water left = _____%

Water used = _____%

48. Of the 100 children who visited the zoo, 35 are girls.

What percent of the children are girls? _____%

What percent of the children are boys? _____%

49.   Of the 100 books borrowed by students, 76 are English books.

What percent of the books are English books? _____%

What percent of the books are not English books? _____%

Solve.

50.   What percent of the fruits are pears?

Complete the model with the words *Fruits* and *Pears*.

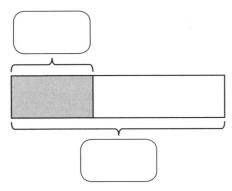

51.   What percent of the visitors are adults?

Complete the model with the words *Visitors* and *Adults*.

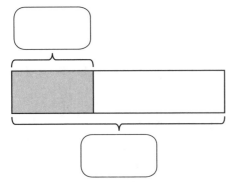

Worksheet 2   Converting Fractions to Percents

Express each fraction as a percent.

> *Example*
>
> $$\frac{23}{50} = \frac{\boxed{46}}{100}$$
>
> $$= \underline{\quad 46 \quad}\%$$

1. $$\frac{11}{20} = \frac{\boxed{}}{100}$$

    $$= \underline{\qquad}\%$$

2. $$\frac{47}{50} = \frac{\boxed{}}{100}$$

    $$= \underline{\qquad}\%$$

3. $$\frac{3}{5} = \frac{\boxed{}}{100}$$

    $$= \underline{\qquad}\%$$

4. $$\frac{3}{4} = \frac{\boxed{}}{100}$$

    $$= \underline{\qquad}\%$$

5. $$\frac{17}{25} = \frac{\boxed{}}{100}$$

    $$= \underline{\qquad}\%$$

Express each fraction as a percent.

Example

$$\frac{7}{25} = \underline{\quad \frac{7}{25} \quad} \times \underline{\quad 1 \quad}$$

$$= \underline{\quad \frac{7}{25} \quad} \times \underline{\quad 100 \quad}\%$$

$$= \underline{\quad 28 \quad}\%$$

---

6. $\frac{31}{50} = \underline{\qquad} \times \underline{\qquad}$

$= \underline{\qquad} \times \underline{\qquad}\%$

$= \underline{\qquad}\%$

7. $\frac{9}{20} = \underline{\qquad} \times \underline{\qquad}$

$= \underline{\qquad} \times \underline{\qquad}\%$

$= \underline{\qquad}\%$

Express each fraction as a percent.

Example

$$\frac{66}{300} = \frac{\boxed{22}}{100} = \underline{\quad 22 \quad}\%$$

---

8. $\frac{44}{200} = \frac{\boxed{}}{100} = \underline{\qquad}\%$

9. $\frac{68}{400} = \frac{\boxed{}}{100} = \underline{\qquad}\%$

10. $\dfrac{125}{500} = \dfrac{\boxed{}}{100} =$ _____ %

11. $\dfrac{424}{800} = \dfrac{\boxed{}}{100} =$ _____ %

Express each fraction as a percent.

> **Example**
>
> $\dfrac{3}{10}$
>
> 10 parts ⟶ 100%
>
> 1 part ⟶ _____10_____ %
>
> 3 parts ⟶ _____30_____ %
>
> $\dfrac{3}{10} =$ _____30_____ %

12. $\dfrac{13}{20}$

20 parts ⟶ 100%

1 part ⟶ _____ %

13 parts ⟶ _____ %

$\dfrac{13}{20} =$ _____ %

13. $\dfrac{9}{25}$

25 parts ⟶ 100%

1 part ⟶ _____ %

9 parts ⟶ _____ %

$\dfrac{9}{25} =$ _____ %

Solve.

14. Sam completed $\frac{7}{25}$ of his homework.

What percent of his homework is not completed?

25 units ⟶ 100%

1 unit ⟶ _____%

7 units ⟶ _____%

Homework completed = _____%

Homework not completed = _____%

15. Kenneth did $\frac{4}{5}$ of his homework.

a. What percent of his homework did Kenneth do?

b. What percent of his homework was left undone?

16. Last year, $\frac{18}{25}$ of Ahmad's land was planted with mango trees. The rest of the land was planted with orange trees. What percent of Ahmad's land was planted with orange trees?

17. Yuri walked $\frac{1}{4}$ of her journey. She cycled for $\frac{1}{5}$ of her journey. What percent of her journey did Yuri not complete?

_____ + _____ = _____

Fraction of journey completed = _____

_____ units ⟶ 100%

1 unit ⟶ _____%

_____ units ⟶ _____%

Percent of journey not completed = _____%

18. Rob had a basket of fruits. Of the fruits, $\frac{1}{3}$ were apples and $\frac{5}{12}$ were oranges. The rest were pears. What percent of the fruits were pears?

19. Serena gave $\frac{1}{2}$ of her pizza to Tina and $\frac{1}{4}$ to Andrew. What percent of the pizza was left?

Worksheet 3   Percent of a Number

Find each answer.

Example

$$100\% \longrightarrow 50$$

$$1\% \longrightarrow \frac{50}{100} = 0.5$$

$$30\% \longrightarrow \underline{0.5 \times 30 = 15}$$

---

1. $100\% \longrightarrow 30$

$1\% \longrightarrow$ _____

$50\% \longrightarrow$ _____

2. $100\% \longrightarrow 40$

$1\% \longrightarrow$ _____

$60\% \longrightarrow$ _____

Example

25% of 280

$$= \underline{\quad \frac{25}{100} \quad} \times \underline{\quad 280 \quad}$$

$$= \underline{\quad 70 \quad}$$

---

3.   70% of 150

$$= \underline{\qquad\quad} \times \underline{\qquad\quad}$$

$$= \underline{\qquad\quad}$$

4.   45% of 320

$$= \underline{\qquad\quad} \times \underline{\qquad\quad}$$

$$= \underline{\qquad\quad}$$

Name: _____ **Date:** _____

Solve these problems using two methods.

5. There were 480 penguin eggs in a basket. Yesterday, 40% of the eggs hatched. How many eggs hatched?

Method 1:

40% of 480 eggs = _____ × _____

= _____

_____ eggs hatched.

Method 2:

100% ⟶ _____ eggs

1% ⟶ _____ eggs

_____% ⟶ _____ eggs

_____ eggs hatched.

6. Mrs. Smith had $850. She spent 60% of it on gifts for her children. How much did Mrs. Smith spend on the gifts?

Method 1:

Method 2:

7.   A butcher bought 240 kilograms of meat. He sold 15% of the meat
      and kept the rest in a refrigerator.

      a.   What percent of the meat was kept in the refrigerator?

            _____% − _____% = _____%

            _____% of the meat was kept in the refrigerator.

      b.   How many kilograms of meat were kept in the refrigerator?

            Method 1:

            _____% × 240 kg = _____ × 240 kg

                                 = _____ kg

            _____ kilograms of meat were kept in the refrigerator.

Method 2:

$$100\% \longrightarrow \text{_____}$$

$$1\% \longrightarrow \text{_____}$$

$$\text{_____}\% \longrightarrow \text{_____}$$

_____ kilograms of meat were kept in the refrigerator.

Solve. Show your work.

8. There were 800 students in a school. Of the students in the school, 55% were American and 22% were British. The rest were Chinese.

    a. What percent of the students were Chinese?

b. How many students were Chinese?

9. Mr. Anderson's monthly salary was $2,000. He spent 45% of his salary on food, 42% of it on rent, and saved the rest. How much money did Mr. Anderson save?

Worksheet 4   Real-World Problems: Percent

Solve. Show your work.

Example

Joleen has $15,000 in a savings account at Booming Bank. The **interest** rate for the account is 6% per year. Wally Mart is offering a 20% storewide **discount**. Joleen is deciding whether or not to buy a furniture set. The regular price of the furniture set at Wally Mart is $4,700. There is a 7% **sales tax** on the sale price of the furniture set.

a. How much interest will Joleen earn after 1 year (assuming she makes no withdrawals)?

6% of $15,000

$= \dfrac{6}{100} \times \$15,000$

$= \$900$

She will earn $900 in interest after 1 year.

b. How much sales tax would she pay on the furniture set?

20% of $4,700

$= \dfrac{20}{100} \times \$4,700$

$= \$940$

The dollar amount of the discount is $940.

$\$4,700 - \$940 = \$3,760$

7% of $3,760

$= \dfrac{7}{100} \times \$3,760$

$= \$263.20$

She would pay $263.20 sales tax.

---

1. Mr. Taylor puts $1,600 in Value Bank. The interest rate is 4% per year. How much interest will he get after 1 year?

2. Mrs. Benjamin puts $1,200 in Virtue bank. The interest rate is 6% per year.

    a. How much interest will she get after 1 year?

    b. How much money will Mrs. Benjamin have in the bank after 1 year?

3.   Benny bought a DVD recorder for $800. He had to pay 5% sales tax on the DVD recorder. How much sales tax did Benny pay?

4.   The price of a computer was $1,500. Lisa bought the computer and had to pay 5% sales tax on the price.

   a.   How much sales tax did Lisa pay?

   b.   How much did she pay in total?

5. The regular price of a refrigerator was $1,200. Mrs. Williams bought the refrigerator at a discount of 15%. How much was the discount?

6. At a sale, Mrs. Jones bought a piano at a discount of 20%. The regular price of the piano was $4,200.

a. What was the discounted price for the piano?

b. Mrs. Jones paid 5% sales tax on the sale price. How much sales tax did she pay?

CHAPTER 11 Graphs and Probability

Worksheet 1   Making and Interpreting Double Bar Graphs

Use the data in the table to draw a bar graph and answer the questions.

Example

The table shows the types of tickets sold at a school fair.

	10¢	20¢	50¢	$1	$2
Total number of tickets	50	70	200	150	80

Draw a bar graph to show the different types of tickets sold.

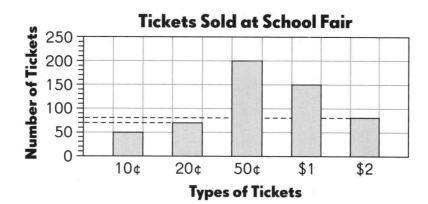

Which ticket is the most popular? _____ 50¢ _____

Which ticket is the least popular? _____ 10¢ _____

How many more $1 tickets than $2 tickets were sold? _____ 70 _____

How many tickets were sold in all? _____ 550 _____

Name: _____ Date: _____

The table shows the number of points scored by students Amy, Ben, Carrie, Danny, Eva, and Flora.

	Amy	Ben	Carrie	Danny	Eva	Flora
Score	7	9	12	6	3	1

Draw a bar graph to show the points scored by each student.

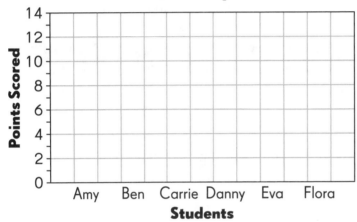

1. Who scores the most points? _____

2. Who scores the fewest points? _____

3. How many more points than Flora does Danny score? _____

4. Who scores three times as many points as Eva? _____

5. How many more points must Amy score so that she gets as many

    points as Carrie? _____

6. How many more points must Eva score so that she gets one point

    fewer than Ben? _____

Name: _____   Date: _____

Use the data in the table to draw a double bar graph and answer the questions.

Example

The table shows the different kinds of toppings that children picked for their ice cream at Jazz Cafe.

	Chocolate		Vanilla		Strawberry		Coffee	
	Boys	Girls	Boys	Girls	Boys	Girls	Boys	Girls
Number	15	12	10	14	8	10	8	6

Draw a **double bar graph** to show the different kinds of toppings picked by the boys and girls for their ice cream.

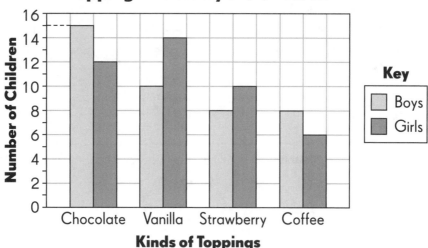

Which topping is the children's favorite? _____Chocolate_____

Which topping is the least popular? _____Coffee_____

How many more children chose the chocolate topping than the

coffee topping? _____13_____

How many children chose the strawberry topping? _____18_____

The table shows the favorite sports of all the students in a school.

	Tennis		Swimming		Softball	
	Boys	Girls	Boys	Girls	Boys	Girls
Number	18	12	24	22	16	8

Draw a double bar graph to show the favorite sports of the boys and girls in the school.

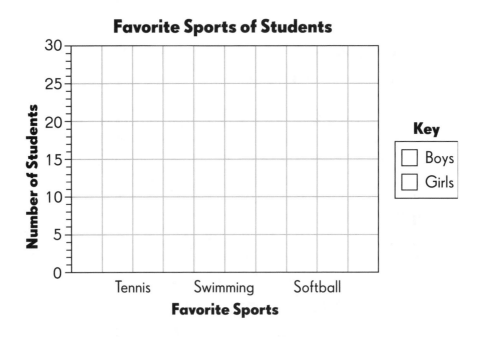

7. How many boys like tennis? _____

8. Do more students prefer softball or swimming? _____

How many more? _____

9. Which is the most popular sport? _____

10. Which is the least popular sport? _____

11. How many girls are there in the school? _____

12. How many boys are there in the school? _____

The table shows the number of fruits picked by Chris and Larry at a farm.

	Apples		Oranges		Pears	
	Chris	**Larry**	**Chris**	**Larry**	**Chris**	**Larry**
Number	80	100	75	45	90	60

Draw a double bar graph.

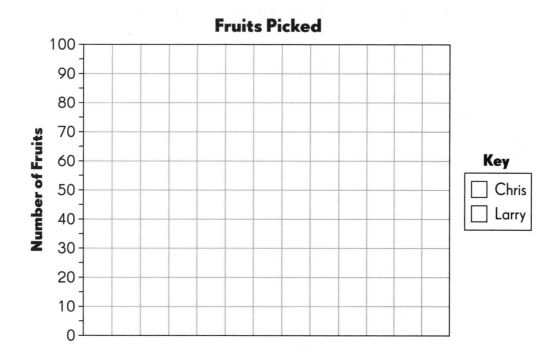

Fruits Picked

Key
☐ Chris
☐ Larry

13. How many fruits did Chris pick? _____

14.   Who picked more fruits, Chris or Larry? _____

How many more? _____

15.   Which type of fruit do Chris and Larry have the greatest

number of? Chris: _____; Larry: _____

16.   Which type of fruit do they have the least number of? _____

17.   How many more oranges must Chris pick so that he has twice as many

oranges as Larry? _____

18.   How many more apples must Larry pick so that Chris has half as many

apples as Larry? _____

Name: _____   **Date:** _____

Worksheet 2   Graphing an Equation

Write the ordered pair for each point.

Example

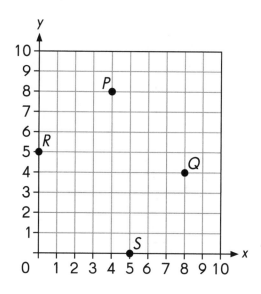

origin

A (____3____, ____9____)   B (____9____, ____3____)

C (____3____, ____0____)   D (____0____, ____2____)

1.   P (_____, _____)   **2.**   Q (_____, _____)

3.   R (_____, _____)   **4.**   S (_____, _____)

Plot each point on the coordinate grid.

Example

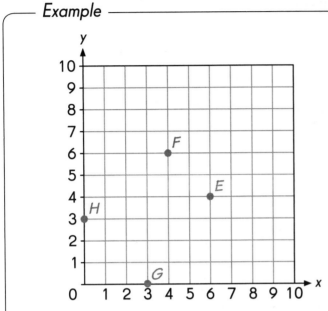

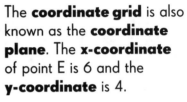
The **coordinate grid** is also known as the **coordinate plane**. The **x-coordinate** of point E is 6 and the **y-coordinate** is 4.

E (6, 4)   F (4, 6)

G (3, 0)   H (0, 3)

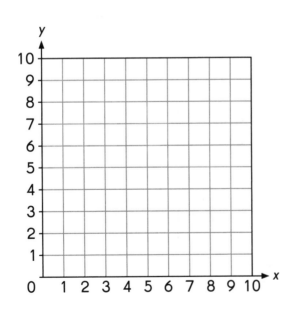

5.   T (3, 5)   **6.**   U (5, 3)

7.   V (7, 0)   **8.**   W (0, 7)

Use the data in the table to plot the graph and answer the questions.

Mandy needs flavored syrup to make drinks for her party guests. The table shows the number of bottles of syrup needed for the number of guests at a party.

Number of bottles of syrup	1	2	3	4	5
Number of guests	8	16	24	32	40

Number of Bottles Needed

9. How many bottles of syrup does Mandy need when there are

24 guests? _____

10. How many bottles of syrup does she need when a total of 30 guests

are at the party? _____

11. Mandy used 2.5 bottles of syrup for a party she held last month.

How many guests were there? _____

12. Mandy has 1.5 bottles of syrup left. How many guests can she invite

to her next party? _____

13. Mandy invites 20 guests to a party. Later that night, 15 more uninvited

guests arrived. How many more bottles of syrup does she need? _____

Use the data in the table to plot the graph and answer the questions.

The table shows two children's savings over five weeks.

	Week 1	Week 2	Week 3	Week 4	Week 5
Jacob	$6	$12	$18	$24	$30
Sarah	$8	$16	$24	$32	$40

14. In which week were Jacob's savings $6 less than Sarah's savings?

_____

15. How much more were Sarah's savings than Jacob's savings after four weeks?

$_____

16. How much did Jacob and Sarah earn in all after five weeks? $_____

17. If Jacob and Sarah saved the same amount of money in Week 6 as they did in the previous weeks, how much would their savings be in Week 6?

Jacob's savings: $_____; Sarah's savings: $_____

18. After Week 5, Sarah bought her brother a birthday gift worth half her savings. Who has a greater amount in his or her savings now? By how much?

$_____; $_____

Worksheet 3 Combinations

Complete.

Example

Joanne has a black blazer, a brown blazer, and a grey blazer.
She has a beige skirt, a tan skirt, and a black skirt.
Make an **organized list** of the possible **combinations** of a blazer
and skirt that Joanne can wear.
Draw a **tree diagram** to show the number of combinations.

Blazer	Skirt	Combinations
Black	Beige	Black/Beige
	Tan	Black/Tan
	Black	Black/Black
Brown	Beige	Brown/Beige
	Tan	Brown/Tan
	Black	Brown/Black
Grey	Beige	Grey/Beige
	Tan	Grey/Tan
	Black	Grey/Black

Blazers   Skirts   Combinations

black   — beige   black/beige
        — tan   black/tan
        — black   black/black

brown   — beige   brown/beige
        — tan   brown/tan
        — black   brown/black

grey   — beige   grey/beige
        — tan   grey/tan
        — black   grey/black

1. Jack has a pair of red socks, a pair of black socks, and a pair of green socks. He has 1 blue tie and 1 brown tie. Make an organized list of the possible combinations of a tie and a pair of socks.

Socks	Ties	Combinations

There are _____ combinations.

2. Kim eats yogurt and fruit every day in different combinations.

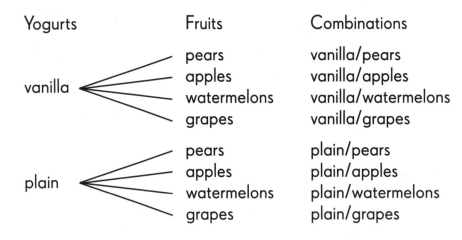

Yogurts	Fruits	Combinations
vanilla	pears	vanilla/pears
	apples	vanilla/apples
	watermelons	vanilla/watermelons
	grapes	vanilla/grapes
plain	pears	plain/pears
	apples	plain/apples
	watermelons	plain/watermelons
	grapes	plain/grapes

Study the tree diagram.

How many types of fruit does Kim eat? _____

How many types of yogurt does she eat? _____

3. Jill drinks either coffee or tea after a meal. She can choose to have cheese, biscuits, or fruit to go with her drink.

a. Draw a tree diagram to show the number of combinations that she can have.

b. How many combinations are there in all?

4.   XYZ supermarket sells 4 choices of cheese, 5 choices of milk, and 6 choices of crackers.

    a.   There are _____ combinations of choosing one type of cheese and one type of milk.

    b.   There are _____ combinations of choosing one type of milk and one type of crackers.

    c.   There are _____ combinations of choosing one type of cheese and one type of crackers.

Name: _____ **Date:** _____

Worksheet 4   Theoretical Probability and Experimental Probability

Complete.

Example

Sandra makes a spinner.

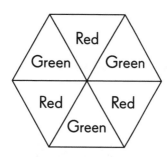

What is the theoretical and the experimental probability of an event happening?

Theoretical probability $= \dfrac{\text{number of favorable outcomes}}{\text{total number of possible outcomes}}$

Experimental probability $= \dfrac{\text{number of \textbf{favorable outcomes}} \text{ in an actual experiment}}{\text{total number of trials}}$

Find the theoretical probability of landing on the red section if the spinner is spun once.

Theoretical probability of landing on the red section $= \dfrac{3}{6} = \dfrac{1}{2}$

Jamil tosses two coins. The coins land on either a head or a tail.
(H, T) shows a head on the first coin and a tail on the second coin.

1.   Write down all possible outcomes. How many outcomes are there in all?

2.   What is the theoretical probability of landing a head and a tail?

3.   What is the theoretical probability of landing two heads?

4.   What is the theoretical probability of landing two tails?

Jess tosses a coin and a cube that is numbered 1 through 6 on its faces.
(H, 5) shows a head on the coin and a 5 on the cube.

5.   Write down all possible outcomes. How many outcomes are there in all?

6.   What is the theoretical probability of getting a head and an even number?

7.   What is the theoretical probability of getting a tail and a number less than 5?

8.   What is the theoretical probability of getting a head and a number greater than 3?

© 2009 Marshall Cavendish International (Singapore) Private Limited. Copying is permitted; see page ii.

Sarah tosses a coin 100 times and she gets a head 45 times and a tail 55 times.

9. Find the experimental probability of getting a head.

10. Find the experimental probability of getting a tail.

11. Jenny and Trish throw a cube that is numbered 1 through 6 on its faces. The cube is thrown 45 times by each girl. Use the data in the table to find the experimental probability of each girl getting each number. Complete the table.

Number	Jenny's outcomes	Experimental probability	Trish's outcomes	Experimental probability
1	8		7	
2	9		8	
3	8		8	
4	6		7	
5	5		6	
6	9		9	

12. Harris makes a spinner that has 4 equal parts. Two parts are painted red, one part is painted green, and one part is painted yellow. He spins the spinner a number of times and obtains these experimental probabilities.

Red 0.52   Green 0.25   Yellow 0.23

What could be the total number of times he spins the spinner?
There is more than one correct answer.
Using your total number of spins, find the number of times the spinner lands on each color.

12 Angles

Worksheet 1 Angles on a Line

Solve.

Example

The **sum of angle measures** on a **line** is 180°.

a. Name the **angles** on line *PR*.
Is $\overrightarrow{QX}$ **perpendicular** to $\overleftrightarrow{PR}$?

b. Name the **angles** on line *AC*.
Is $\overrightarrow{BD}$ **perpendicular** to $\overleftrightarrow{AC}$?

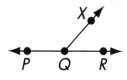
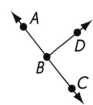

a. ∠*PQX* and ∠*XQR*
$\overrightarrow{QX}$ is not perpendicular to $\overleftrightarrow{PR}$ as m∠*PQX* is not equal to 90°.

b. ∠*ABD* and ∠*DBC*
$\overrightarrow{BD}$ is perpendicular to $\overleftrightarrow{AC}$ as m∠*ABD* = 90°.

---

1. Study the figure on the right and find the line.
Check your answer by using a protractor.
Then add up the angle measures on the line.

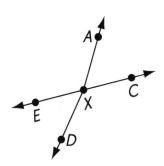

_____ is a line because

m∠_____ + m∠_____ = 180°.

Measure $\angle a$ using a protractor. Find the measure of $\angle b$.

Example

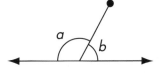

$m\angle a + m\angle b = 180°$

$m\angle a = \underline{\quad 35° \quad}$

$m\angle b$

$= 180° - m\angle a$

$= 180° - \underline{\quad 35° \quad}$

$= \underline{\quad 145° \quad}$

2.

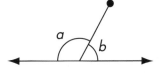

$m\angle a + m\angle b = 180°$

$m\angle a = \underline{\qquad\qquad}$

$m\angle b$

$= 180° - \underline{\qquad\qquad}$

$= \underline{\qquad\qquad}$

3.

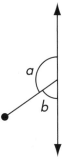

$m\angle a + m\angle b = 180°$

$m\angle a = \underline{\qquad\qquad}$

$m\angle b$

$= \underline{\qquad\qquad} - \underline{\qquad\qquad}$

$= \underline{\qquad\qquad}$

$\overleftrightarrow{AB}$ **is a line. Find the measure of each unknown angle.**

4.

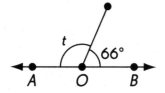

m∠t

= _____ − 66°

= _____

5.

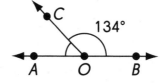

m∠AOC

= _____ − _____

= _____

∠ABC is a right angle. Measure ∠x using a protractor. Find the measure of ∠y.

6.

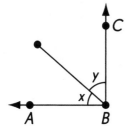

m∠x + m∠y = 90°

m∠x = _____

m∠y = 90° − m∠x

= 90° − _____

= _____

7.

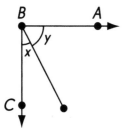

m∠x + m∠y = 90°

m∠x = _____

m∠y = 90° − m∠x

= 90° − _____

= _____

$\overrightarrow{AB}$ **is perpendicular to** $\overrightarrow{BC}$ **. Find the measure of each unknown angle.**

8.

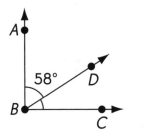

   m∠DBC

   = _____ − _____

   = _____

9.

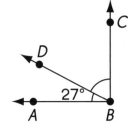

   m∠CBD

   = _____ − _____

   = _____

$\overleftrightarrow{AB}$ **is perpendicular to** $\overrightarrow{CD}$ **. Find the measure of each unknown angle.**

10.

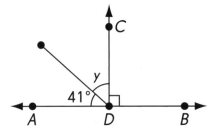

   m∠y + 41° + 90° = 180°

   m∠y + _____ = 180°

   m∠y = _____ − _____

   = _____

© 2009 Marshall Cavendish International (Singapore) Private Limited. Copying is permitted; see page ii.

11.

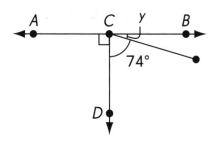

$m\angle y + 74° + 90° = 180°$

$m\angle y + \underline{\hspace{2cm}} = 180°$

$m\angle y = \underline{\hspace{1.5cm}} - \underline{\hspace{1.5cm}}$

$= \underline{\hspace{1.5cm}}$

12. $\overleftrightarrow{AB}$ is a line. ADC is a right angle. Find the measure of $\angle x$.

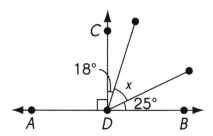

Complete.

13. $\overleftrightarrow{AC}$ is a line. Find the measure of $\angle x$.

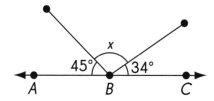

14. Circle the cards which contain the angle measures that add up to 180°.

115°

47°   28°

37°   98°

44°

Worksheet 2   Angles at a Point

Complete.
Name the angles at point *O* and state the sum of the measures of the angles.

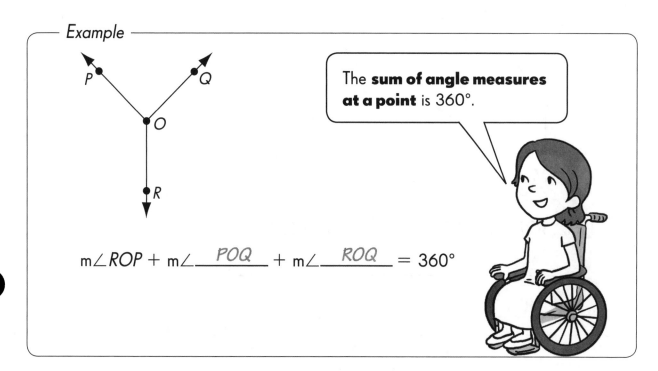

— *Example* —

The **sum of angle measures at a point** is 360°.

m∠*ROP* + m∠___*POQ*___ + m∠___*ROQ*___ = 360°

1.

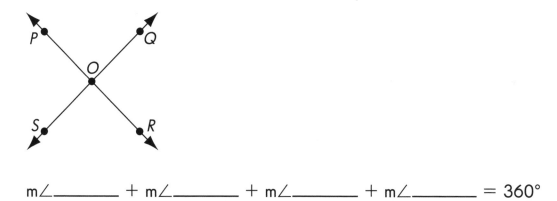

m∠_____ + m∠_____ + m∠_____ + m∠_____ = 360°

Find the measure of the unknown angles using a protractor and state the sum of the measures of the angles.

Example

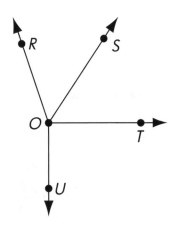

m∠SOT + m∠TOU + m∠SOR + m∠ROU

= ___55°___ + ___90°___ + ___54°___ + ___161°___

= ___360°___

2.

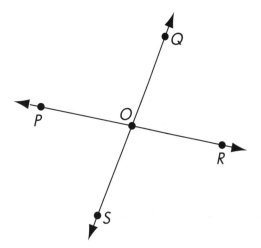

m∠POQ + m∠QOR + m∠ROS + m∠SOP

= _____ + _____ + _____ + _____

= _____

Find the measure of ∠s using a protractor. Find the measure of ∠t.

3.

$m\angle s + m\angle t = 360°$

$m\angle s =$ _____

$m\angle t = 360° - m\angle s$

$\quad = 360° -$ _____

$\quad =$ _____

4.

$m\angle s + m\angle t = 360°$

$m\angle s =$ _____

$m\angle t = 360° - m\angle s$

$\quad = 360° -$ _____

$\quad =$ _____

Find the measure of the unknown angle.

5.

115°

x

$m\angle x$

$= $ _____ $- 115°$

$=$ _____

6.

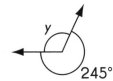

y

245°

$m\angle y$

$=$ _____ $-$ _____

$=$ _____

Complete.

7. $\overleftrightarrow{AB}$ and $\overleftrightarrow{CD}$ are lines. Find the measures of ∠x, ∠y, and ∠z.

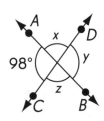

8.   Find the measure of ∠x.

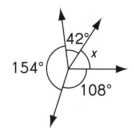

9. $\overleftrightarrow{AC}$ is a line. Find the measure of ∠x.

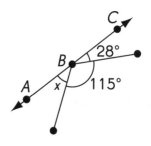

10.   Circle the cards which contain the angle measures that add up to 360°.

70°

180°   145°

85°   220°

130°

Worksheet 3   Vertical Angles

Complete.

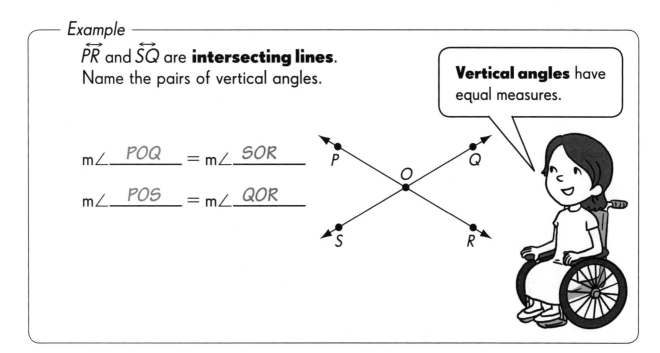

— *Example* —

$\overleftrightarrow{PR}$ and $\overleftrightarrow{SQ}$ are **intersecting lines**.
Name the pairs of vertical angles.

Vertical angles have equal measures.

$m\angle\underline{\quad POQ \quad} = m\angle\underline{\quad SOR \quad}$

$m\angle\underline{\quad POS \quad} = m\angle\underline{\quad QOR \quad}$

1.   *ABCD* is a square.
Name the pairs of vertical angles.

$m\angle\underline{\qquad\qquad} = m\angle\underline{\qquad\qquad}$

$m\angle\underline{\qquad\qquad} = m\angle\underline{\qquad\qquad}$

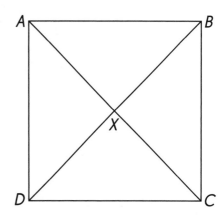

2.   m∠p = m∠r
m∠q = m∠s
Use the above statements to help you name the angles in the diagram.
Give two possible answers.

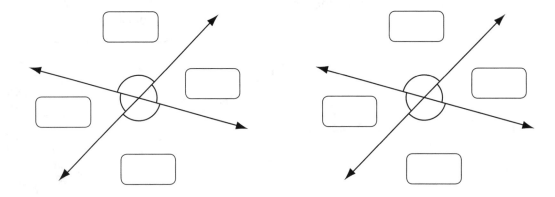

3.

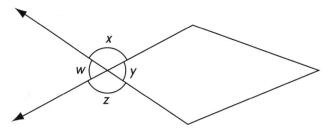

Look at the diagram above. Name the marked angles that are vertical angles.

m∠_____ = m∠_____

m∠_____ = m∠_____

4. $\overleftrightarrow{WY}$ and $\overleftrightarrow{XZ}$ are lines.
Find the measures of $\angle YOZ$ and $\angle WOX$.

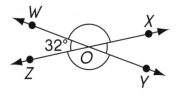

m$\angle YOZ$ = _____°

m$\angle WOX$ = _____°

5. $\overleftrightarrow{AC}$ and $\overleftrightarrow{BD}$ are lines.
Find the measures of $\angle AOD$, $\angle COD$, and $\angle BOC$.

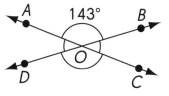

m$\angle AOD$ = _____°

m$\angle COD$ = _____°

m$\angle BOC$ = _____°

6. Find the measure of $\angle x$.

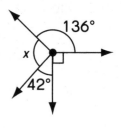

7. $\overleftrightarrow{AB}$ and $\overleftrightarrow{CD}$ are lines. Find the measure of $\angle x$.

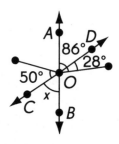

8. $\overleftrightarrow{PS}$, $\overleftrightarrow{QT}$, and $\overleftrightarrow{RV}$ are lines.
Find the measures of $\angle UOV$, $\angle TOU$, and $\angle SOT$.

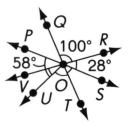

CHAPTER 13 Properties of Triangles and 4-Sided Figures

Worksheet 1   Classifying Triangles

The figures are not drawn to scale.

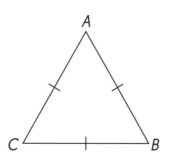

State whether these statements are _true_ or _false_.

Triangle *ABC* is an equilateral triangle.

1.   Any two sides are equal.   _____

2.   All the angles measure 60°.   _____

3.   A right triangle can also be an equilateral triangle.   _____

4.   An equilateral triangle can also be an isosceles triangle.   _____

5.   An isosceles triangle can never be an equilateral triangle.   _____

Put a check in the box if the triangle is an equilateral triangle.

6.
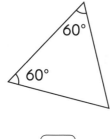

7.
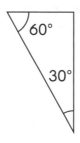

8.
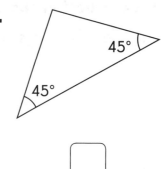

The figures are not drawn to scale.

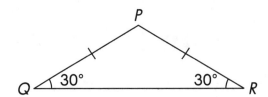

State whether these statements are *true* or *false*.

Triangle *PQR* is an isosceles triangle.

9.   Two sides are equal.   _____

10.   Any two angles are equal.   _____

11.   A triangle with three equal sides can also be an isosceles triangle.   _____

12.   A right triangle can also be an isosceles triangle.   _____

Put a check in the box if the triangle is an isosceles triangle.

13.      **14.**   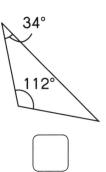   **15.**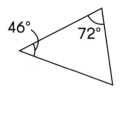

☐   ☐   ☐

State whether these statements are *true* or *false*.

Triangle *WXY* is a scalene triangle.

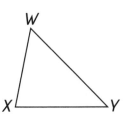

16.   All three sides are of different lengths.   _____

17.   All three angle measures are different.   _____

Name: _____   Date: _____

Put a check in the box if the triangle is a scalene triangle.

18.
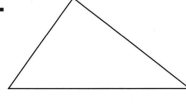
☐

19.
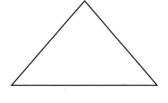
☐

20.
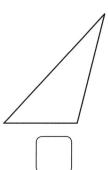
☐

State whether these statements are *true* or *false*.

Triangle *ABC* is a right triangle.

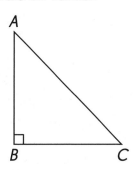

21.   One angle is 90°.   _____

22.   The sum of any two angle measures is 90°.   _____

23.   The sum of all the angle measures is 90°.   _____

Put a check in the box if the triangle is a right triangle.

24.
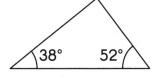
☐

25.
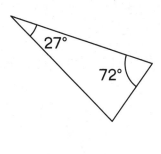
☐

26.
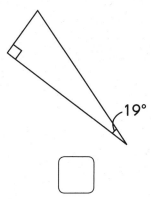
☐

The figures are not drawn to scale.

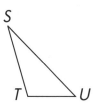

State whether these statements are *true* or *false*.

Triangle *STU* is an obtuse triangle.

27. All the angles measure less than 90°. _____

28. An obtuse triangle can also be an isosceles or a scalene triangle. _____

Put a check in the box if the triangle is an obtuse triangle.

29.

30.

31.

State whether these statements are *true* or *false*.

Triangle *PQR* is an acute triangle.

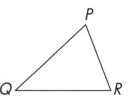

32. All the angles measure greater than 90°. _____

33. An acute triangle can also be an equilateral, isosceles, or scalene triangle. _____

Put a check in the box if the triangle is an acute triangle.

34.

35.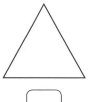

36.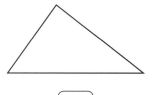

© 2009 Marshall Cavendish International (Singapore) Private Limited. Copying is permitted; see page ii.

Worksheet 2   Measures of Angles of a Triangle

The figures are not drawn to scale.

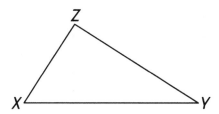

State whether these statements are true or false.

Triangle *XYZ* has three unequal sides.

1.   ∠*X*, ∠*Y*, and ∠*Z* are the three angles of the triangle.   _____

2.   The sum of the measures of ∠*X*, ∠*Y*, and ∠*Z* is 180°.   _____

3.   All the angles must measure less than 90°.   _____

4.   At most one angle measure is equal to or greater than 90°.   _____

Complete. Find the unknown angle measures.

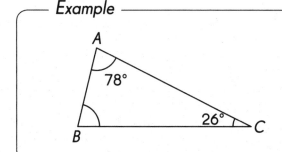

Example

m∠*B* = ___76°___

5.

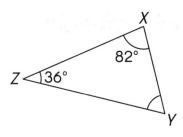

$m\angle Y =$ _____

6.

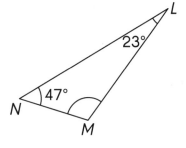

$m\angle M =$ _____

7.

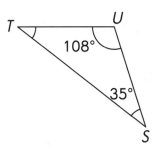

$m\angle T =$ _____

8. $\overline{PR}$ is a line segment. Find the measure of $\angle PQS$.

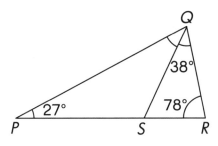

9. $\overline{AC}$ is a line segment. Find the measure of $\angle BDC$.

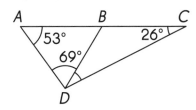

10.   *ABC* is a right triangle.

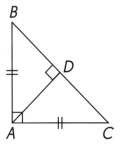

a.   Find the measure of ∠*C*.

b. $\overline{AD}$ is perpendicular to $\overline{BC}$ at *D*. Find the measure of ∠*DAC*.

Complete.

11.

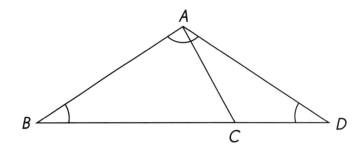

m∠_____ + m∠_____ + m∠_____ = 180°

State whether these statements are true or false.

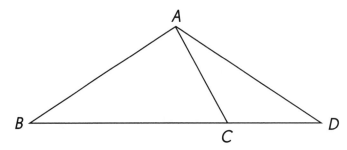

12.   m∠ABC + m∠BAC + m∠BCA = 90°   _____

13.   m∠ADC + m∠DAC + m∠BAC + m∠ABC = 180°   _____

14.   m∠ADC + m∠DAC + m∠ACD = 180°   _____

Complete.

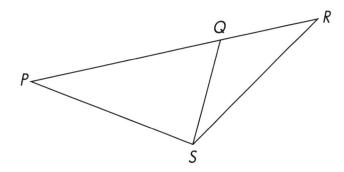

Write 3 sets of angles that total 180°.

15. | m∠ | | m∠ | | m∠ |

16. | m∠ | | m∠ | | m∠ |

17. | m∠ | | m∠ | | m∠ |

Write a set of 4 angles that total 180°.

18. | m∠ | | m∠ | | m∠ | | m∠ |

Triangle *ABC* is not drawn to scale.

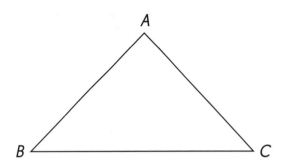

Write true or false for each statement.

19. If $m\angle B + m\angle C = 90°$, then $m\angle A$ is 90°.   _____

20. If $m\angle A = 90°$, then $m\angle B$ is less than 90°.   _____

Write 3 different possible measures for $\angle B$ and $\angle C$.

21. If $m\angle A = 80°$, then $m\angle B =$ _____ $m\angle C =$ _____

22. If $m\angle A = 80°$, then $m\angle B =$ _____ $m\angle C =$ _____

23. If $m\angle A = 80°$, then $m\angle B =$ _____ $m\angle C =$ _____

Name: _____   **Date:** _____

Worksheet 3   Right, Isosceles, and Equilateral Triangles

Find the unknown angle measure in each right triangle.

Example

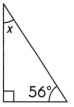

This is a **right triangle**.

$m\angle x =$ ___34___ °

1.

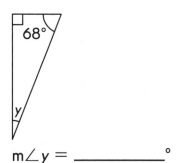

68°

y

$m\angle y =$ _____ °

2.

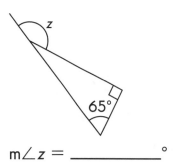

z

65°

$m\angle z =$ _____ °

Find the unknown angle measure in each isosceles triangle.

Example

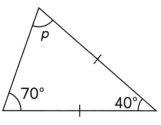

p

70°   40°

This is an **isosceles triangle**.

$m\angle p =$ ___70___ °

3.

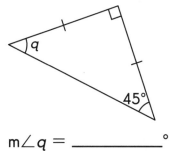

q

45°

$m\angle q =$ _____ °

4.

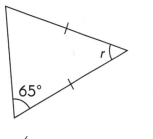

65°   r

$m\angle r =$ _____ °

Find the unknown angle measure(s) in each isosceles triangle.

Example

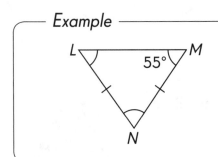

$m\angle MLN =$ _____55_____ °

$m\angle LNM =$ _____70_____ °

5.

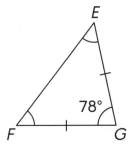

$m\angle FEG =$ _____ °

$m\angle EFG =$ _____ °

6. $\overrightarrow{PS}$ is a ray.

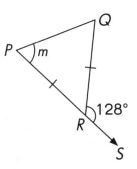

$m\angle m =$ _____ °

7. $\overrightarrow{AC}$ is a ray.

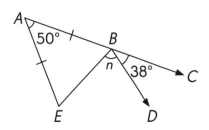

$m\angle n =$ _____ °

8.   *ABC* is an isosceles triangle with sides *AB* = *AC*.

    a.   m∠*A* = 70°
        Find the measure of ∠*C*.

    b.   Point *D* is on segment *BC*. $\overline{AD}$ is perpendicular to $\overline{BC}$.
        Find the measure of ∠*DAC*.

9.   *ABC* is an isosceles triangle with sides *AB* = *AC*.

    a.   m∠*A* = 105°
        Find the measure of ∠*C*.

    b.   Point *D* is on segment *BC*.
        m∠*DAC* = 25°
        Find the measure of ∠*ADB*.

Find the unknown angle measure(s).

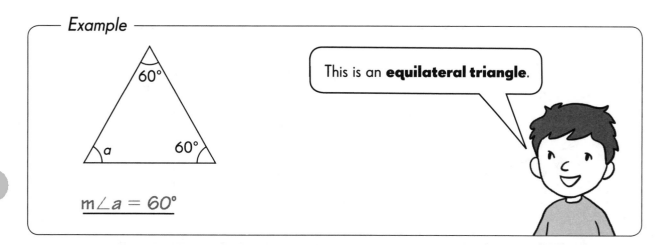

Example

This is an **equilateral triangle**.

m∠*a* = 60°

10.

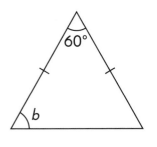

_____

11.

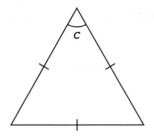

_____

12.

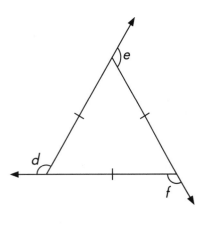

_____

13.

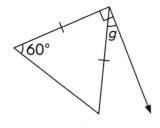

_____

14.

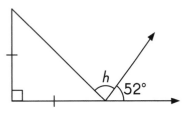

_____

15.

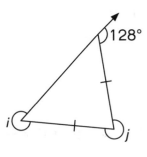

_____

16.

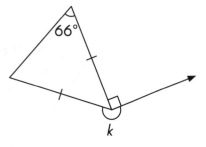

_____

17.

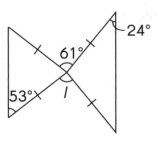

_____

Worksheet 4   Triangle Inequalities

The figure is not drawn to scale.

Example

Complete.

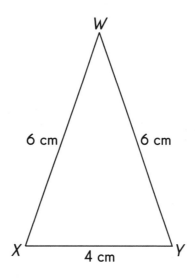

$WX =$ _____6_____ cm

$WY =$ _____6_____ cm

$XY + WY =$ _____10_____ cm

$XY =$ _____4_____ cm

$WX + XY =$ _____10_____ cm

$WX + WY =$ _____12_____ cm

Look at the triangle *WXY*. Fill in the blanks with *Yes* or *No*.

Is $WX + XY > WY$? _____Yes_____

Is $XY + WY > WX$? _____Yes_____

Is $WX + WY > XY$? _____Yes_____

These are **inequalities**.

The figure is not drawn to scale.
Complete.

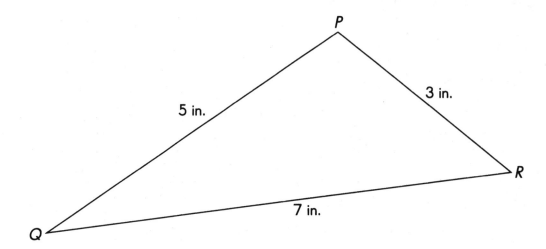

1. $PQ =$ _____ in.

2. $QR =$ _____ in.

3. $PR =$ _____ in.

4. $PQ + QR =$ _____ in.

5. $QR + PR =$ _____ in.

6. $PQ + PR =$ _____ in.

Look at the triangle *PQR*. Fill in the blanks with *Yes* or *No*.

7. Is $PQ + QR > PR$? _____

8. Is $QR + PR > PQ$? _____

9. Is $PQ + PR > QR$? _____

Show whether it is possible to form triangles with these sides.

10.   2 in.,   3 in.,   5 in.

11.   4 cm,   5 cm,   10 cm

12.   6 cm,   7 cm,   8 cm

Find all the possible lengths for the missing side. The lengths are in whole centimeters or whole inches.

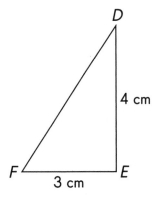

─── Example ───

DF is greater than 4 centimeters.

What are the possible lengths of $\overline{DF}$?

$DE + EF = 4$ cm $+ 3$ cm
$\qquad\qquad = 7$ cm
$DE + EF > DF$
7 cm $> DF$

So, DF is greater than 4 centimeters and less than 7 centimeters. The possible lengths of DF are 5 centimeters and 6 centimeters.

13. In triangle ABC, $AB = 5$ inches, $BC = 6$ inches, and AC is greater than 4 inches. What are the possible lengths of $\overline{AC}$?

14. XYZ is a triangle in which $XY = 11$ centimeters and $YZ = 15$ centimeters. The length of XZ is in whole centimeters and is greater than 20 centimeters. What are the possible lengths of $\overline{XZ}$?

Worksheet 5   Parallelogram, Rhombus, and Trapezoid

The figures are not drawn to scale.

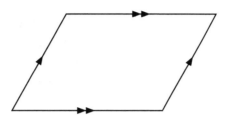

State whether these statements are _true_ or _false_.

The figure is a parallelogram.

1.   All sides are of equal length.   _____

2.   All angle measures are equal.   _____

3.   Opposite sides of the parallelogram are of equal length.   _____

4.   The measures of the opposite angles of the parallelogram
         are equal.   _____

Put a check in the box if the figure is a parallelogram.

5.

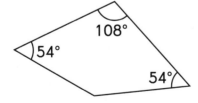

6.

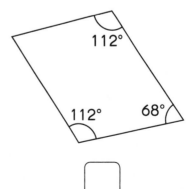

Find the unknown angle measure(s) in each parallelogram.

Example

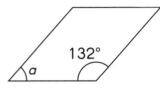

132°

a

This is a **parallelogram**. The opposite sides are parallel.

m∠a = 180° − 132°

= 48°

7.

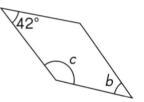

42°

c

b

_____

_____

8.

42°

d

38°

e

_____

_____

9.

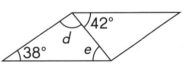

135°

48°

f

g

_____

_____

10.

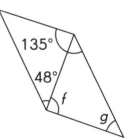

37°

h

39°

i

101°

_____

_____

Name: _____ Date: _____

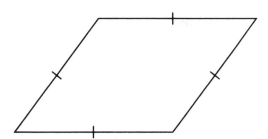

State whether these statements are *true* or *false*.

The figure is a rhombus.

11. All the sides of a rhombus are of equal length. _____

12. All the angle measures of a rhombus are equal. _____

13. Opposite sides of a rhombus are of equal length. _____

14. The measures of the opposite angles of a rhombus are equal. _____

15. A rhombus is also a parallelogram. _____

Put a check in the box if the figure is a rhombus.

16.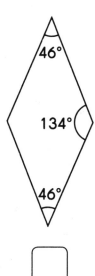

17.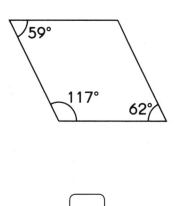

© 2009 Marshall Cavendish International (Singapore) Private Limited. Copying is permitted; see page ii.

Find the unknown angle measure(s) in each rhombus.

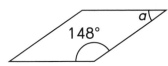

$m\angle a = 180° - 148°$

$= 32°$

A **rhombus** is a special kind of parallelogram.

18.

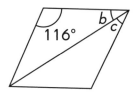

_____

_____

19.

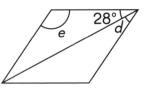

_____

_____

20.

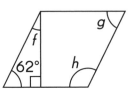

_____

_____

21.

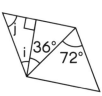

_____

_____

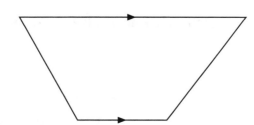

State whether these statements are *true* or *false*.

The figure is a trapezoid.

22.   All the sides of a trapezoid are of equal length.   _____

23.   All the angle measures of a trapezoid are equal.   _____

24.   A trapezoid has only one pair of opposite sides of
          equal length.   _____

25.   A trapezoid has only one pair of opposite angles of
          equal measure.   _____

26.   A trapezoid is also a parallelogram.   _____

Put a check in the box if the figure is a trapeziod.

27.   **28.**

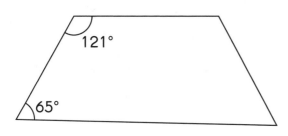

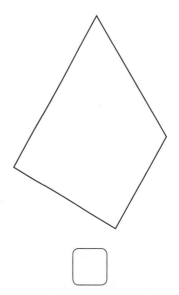

Find the unknown angle measure(s) in each trapezoid.

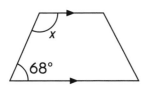

Example

This is a **trapezoid**. One pair of opposite sides is parallel.

m∠x + _____68°_____ = 180°

m∠x = _____180°_____ – _____68°_____

= _____112°_____

29.

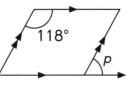

_____

30.

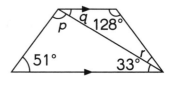

_____

31.

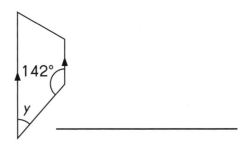

_____

32.

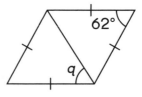

_____

33.

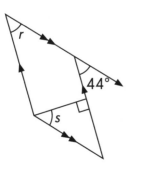

_____

34.

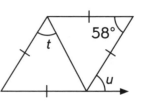

_____

35.

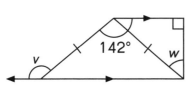

_____

CHAPTER 14 Three-Dimensional Shapes

Worksheet 1   Prisms and Pyramids

Complete.

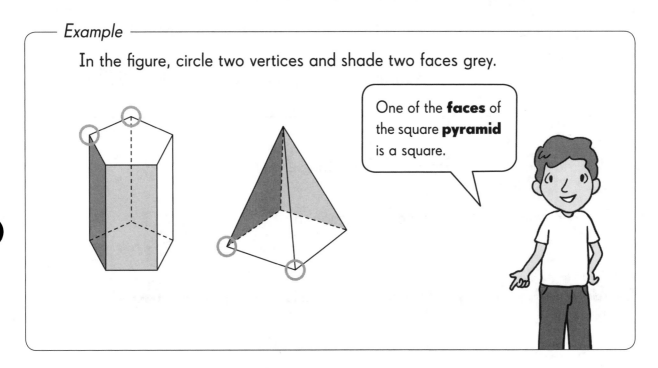

Example

In the figure, circle two vertices and shade two faces grey.

One of the **faces** of the square **pyramid** is a square.

---

1.   In the figure, circle three vertices and color three edges grey.

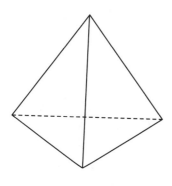

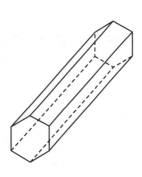

The **triangular pyramid** has 6 **edges**.

Circle the shape(s) that can be found in the figure.

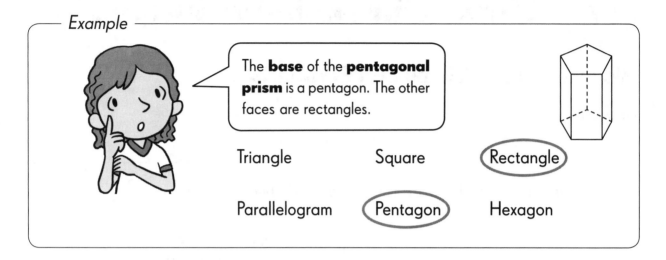

Example

The **base** of the **pentagonal prism** is a pentagon. The other faces are rectangles.

Triangle   Square   (Rectangle)

Parallelogram   (Pentagon)   Hexagon

2.   Triangle   Square   Rectangle

Parallelogram   Pentagon   Hexagon

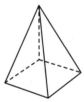

Shade each solid shape if it has two identical and parallel faces.

3.

  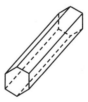

Put a check in the box if the solid figure is a prism.

4.

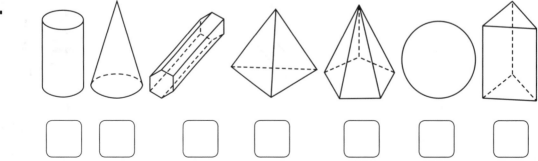

☐   ☐   ☐   ☐   ☐   ☐   ☐

Match the names to the solid figures.

5.

Rectangular prism ●

Pentagonal prism ●

Triangular prism ●

Octagonal prism ●

Hexagonal prism ●

●

●

●

●

●

Complete the table.

Type of prism	Number of faces	Number of edges	Number of vertices
6. Rectangular			
7. Pentagonal			
8. Triangular			
9. Octagonal			
10. Hexagonal			

Put a check in the box if the solid figure is a pyramid.
Shade the base of each pyramid.

11.

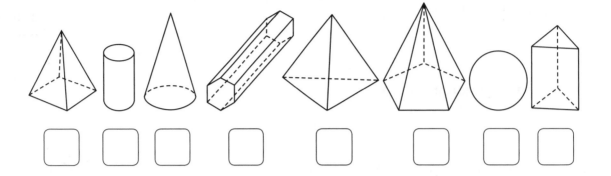

☐ ☐ ☐ ☐ ☐ ☐ ☐ ☐

Match the names to the solid figures.

12.

Triangular pyramid ●

Rectangular pyramid ●

Pentagonal pyramid ●

Hexagonal pyramid ●

Octagonal pyramid ●

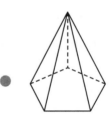

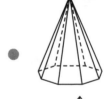

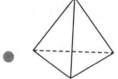

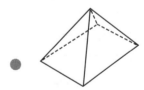

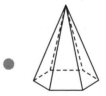

Complete the table.

	Type of pyramid	Number of faces	Number of edges	Number of vertices
13.	Triangular			
14.	Rectangular			
15.	Pentagonal			
16.	Hexagonal			
17.	Octagonal			

These are the nets of some pyramids.
Shade the base of each pyramid.

18.

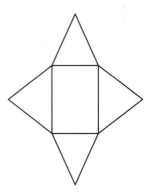

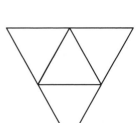

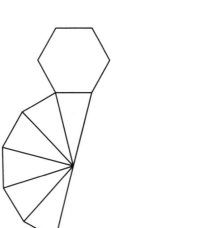

More than one **net** may form the same solid figure.

These are the nets of some prisms. Shade the identical and parallel edges of each prism using different colors.

19.

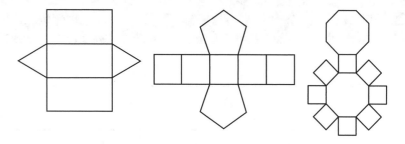

Match the nets with the solid figure they form.

20.

  •   •

  •   •

  •   •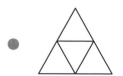

  •   •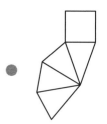

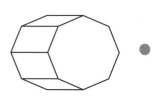 •   •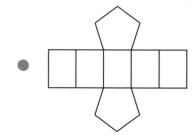

Name: _____   Date: _____

Worksheet 2   Cylinder, Sphere, and Cone

Complete.

1.   In each figure, shade the base and circle the vertex.

2.   In each figure, shade the curved surface green and the flat faces red.

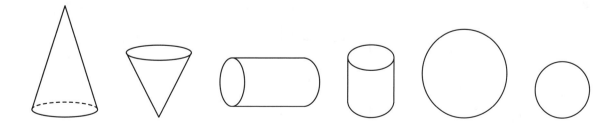

Circle the shape(s) that can be found in the figure.

3.

Circle   Triangle   Square

Rectangle   Parallelogram

4.

Circle   Triangle   Square

Rectangle   Pentagon

Shade each solid shape if it has two identical and parallel faces.

5.

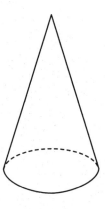
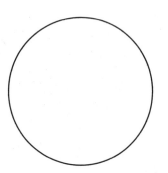

Name: _____   **Date:** _____

Put a check in the box if the solid figure is a cylinder and an ✗ if the solid figure is a cone.

6.

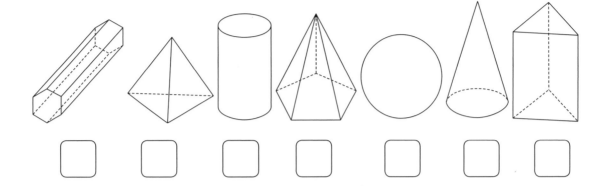

☐ ☐ ☐ ☐ ☐ ☐ ☐

Match the names to the solid figures.

7.

Sphere ●

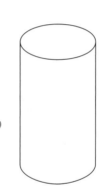
●

Cone ●

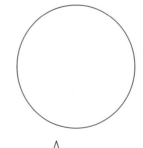
●

Cylinder ●

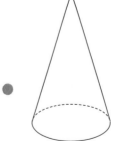
●

BLANK

Surface Area and Volume

Worksheet 1   Building Solids Using Unit Cubes

How many unit cubes are used to build each solid?

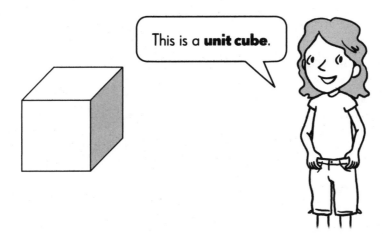

This is a **unit cube**.

1.

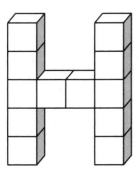

_____ unit cubes

2.

_____ unit cubes

3.

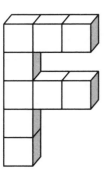

_____ unit cubes

4.

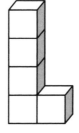

_____ unit cubes

5.

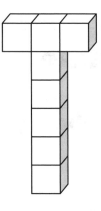

_____ unit cubes

6.

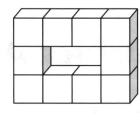

_____ unit cubes

7.

_____ unit cubes

8.

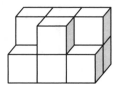

_____ unit cubes

9.   Draw three different solids using 7 unit cubes.

10.   Draw three different solids using 15 unit cubes.

Name: _____ **Date:** _____

Worksheet 2 Drawing Cubes and Rectangular Prisms

Draw these cubes or rectangular prisms on the dot paper without showing the unit cubes.

Example

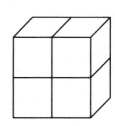
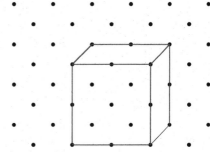

1.

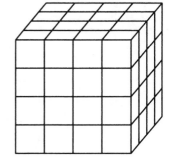

2.

3.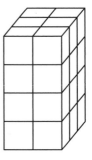

4.

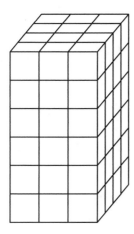

Complete the drawing of each cube or rectangular prism.

5.

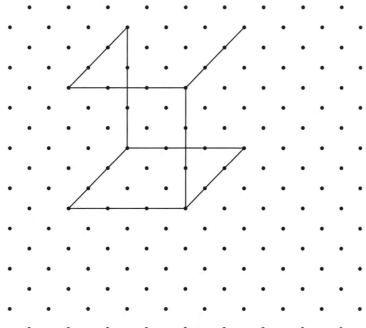

6.

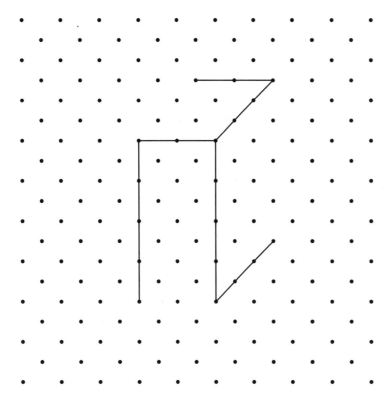

Draw a rectangular prism that has edges 3 times as long as this prism.

7.

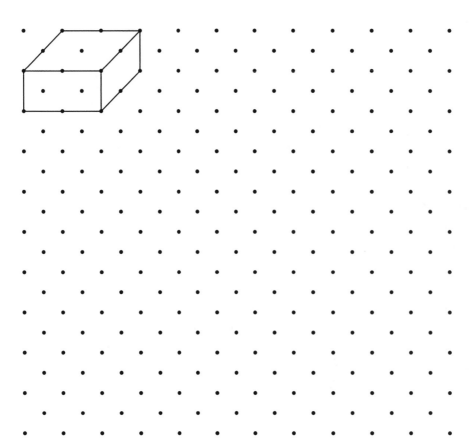

Worksheet 3   Nets and Surface Area

Find the surface area of each cube.

Example

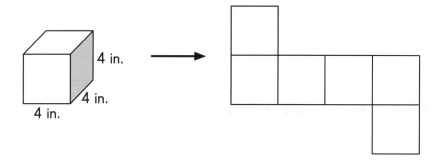

Area of one square face $= 4 \times 4$
$= 16$ in.^{2}

Surface area of the cube $= 6 \times 16$
$= 96$ in.^{2}

The **surface area** is equal to the sum of the areas of the 6 square faces.

1.

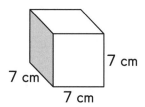

7 cm

7 cm

7 cm

2.

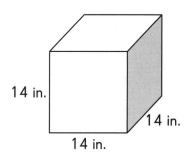

14 in.

14 in.

14 in.

3.

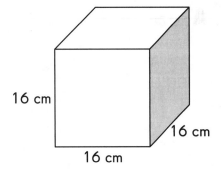

16 cm
16 cm
16 cm

Find the surface area of each rectangular prism.

4.

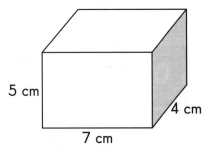

5 cm
4 cm
7 cm

5.

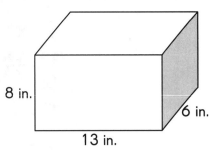

8 in.
6 in.
13 in.

6.

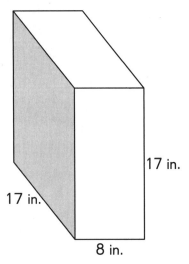

17 in.
17 in.
8 in.

7.

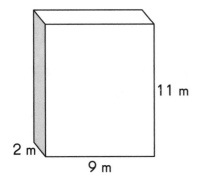

2 m
9 m
11 m

Find the surface area of each triangular prism.

8.

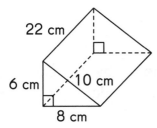

22 cm
6 cm
10 cm
8 cm

The base of this triangular prism is a **right triangle**.

9.

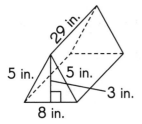

29 in.
5 in.
5 in.
3 in.
8 in.

Solve. Show your work.

10.   A rectangular cupboard measures 110 centimeters by 85 centimeters by
40 centimeters. What is the surface area of the cupboard?

11.   A rectangular display cabinet measures 96 centimeters by 78 centimeters
by 34 centimeters. What is the surface area of the outside of the cabinet
if it does not have a cover?

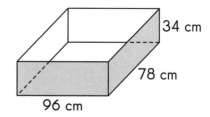

12.   A rectangular bedroom measures 12 feet by $8\frac{1}{2}$ feet by 7 feet. The rectangular
door in the bedroom measures 2 feet by $6\frac{1}{2}$ feet. Joanne decides to paint the
walls of the room pink. Find the surface area of the walls in the room.

Worksheet 4   Understanding and Measuring Volume

These solids are formed by stacking 1-centimeter cubes. Find the volume of each solid.

1.

Volume = _____ cm³

2.

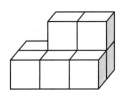

Volume = _____ cm³

3.

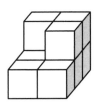

Volume = _____ cm³

4.

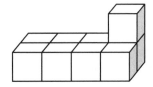

Volume = _____ cm³

5.

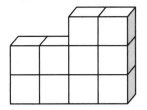

Volume = _____ cm³

6.

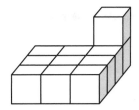

Volume = _____ cm³

7.

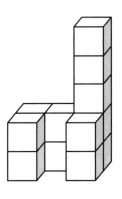

Volume = _____ cm³

8.

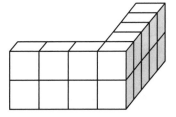

Volume = _____ cm³

These solids are built using unit cubes. Find the volume of each solid. Then compare the volumes and fill in the blanks.

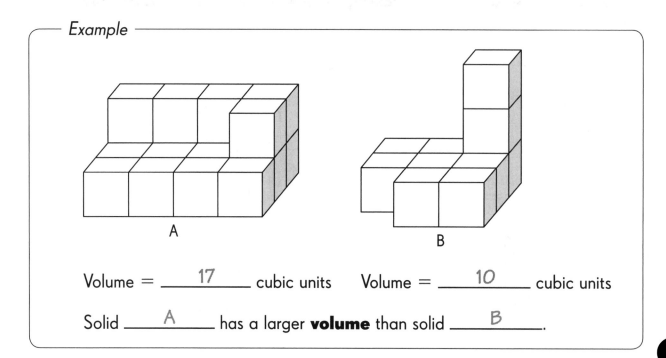

Example

A

B

Volume = _____17_____ cubic units   Volume = _____10_____ cubic units

Solid _____A_____ has a larger **volume** than solid _____B_____.

These solids are built using 1-inch cubes. Find the volume of each solid. Then compare their volumes and fill in the blanks.

9.

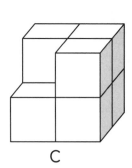

C

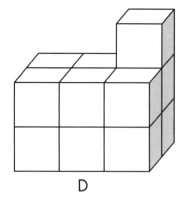

D

Volume = _____ in.³   Volume = _____ in.³

Solid _____ has a smaller volume than solid _____.

Name: _____   Date: _____

These solids are built using 1-foot cubes. Find the volume of each solid. Then compare their volumes and fill in the blanks.

10.

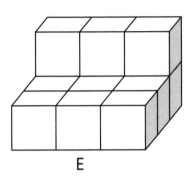

E

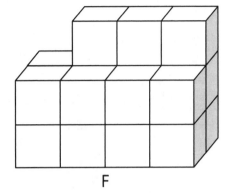

F

Volume = _____ ft³   Volume = _____ ft³

Solid _____ has a larger volume than solid _____.

These solids are built using 1-centimeter cubes. Find the volume of each solid. Then compare their volumes and fill in the blanks.

11.

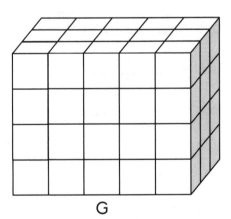

G

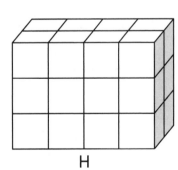

H

Length = _____ cm   Length = _____ cm

Width = _____ cm   Width = _____ cm

Height = _____ cm   Height = _____ cm

Volume = _____ cm³   Volume = _____ cm³

Solid _____ has a larger volume than solid _____.

These solids are built using 1-meter cubes. Find the volume of each solid. Then compare their volumes and fill in the blanks.

12.

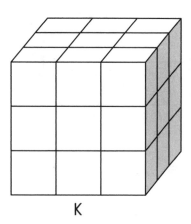

K

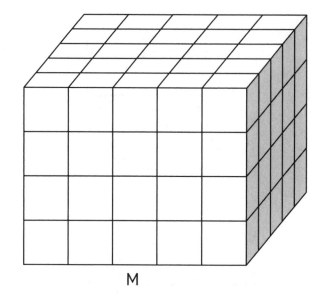

M

Length = _____ m   Length = _____ m

Width = _____ m   Width = _____ m

Height = _____ m   Height = _____ m

Volume = _____ m³   Volume = _____ m³

Solid _____ has a smaller volume than solid _____.

Worksheet 5   Volume of a Rectangular Prism and Liquid

Find the volume of each rectangular prism or cube.

1.

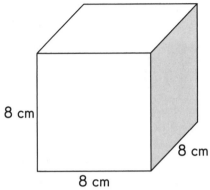

8 cm

8 cm

8 cm

Volume = _____

2.

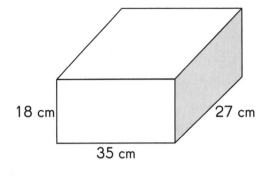

18 cm

27 cm

35 cm

Volume = _____

3.

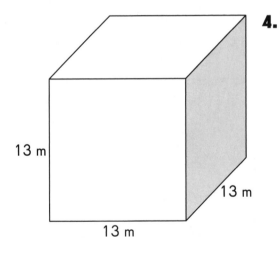

13 m

13 m

13 m

Volume = _____

4.

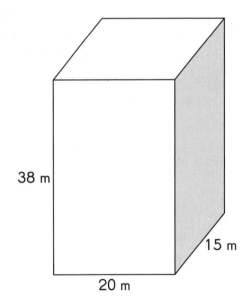

38 m

15 m

20 m

Volume = _____

5.

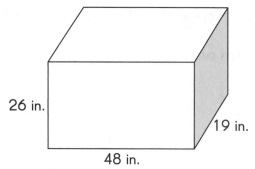

26 in.   19 in.

48 in.

Volume = _____

6.

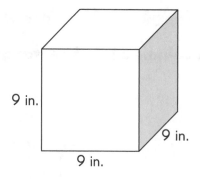

9 in.   9 in.

9 in.

Volume = _____

7.

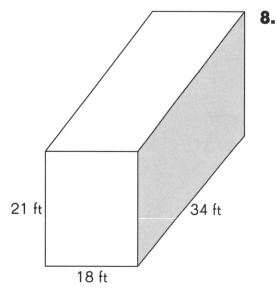

21 ft   34 ft

18 ft

Volume = _____

8.

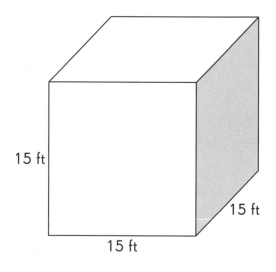

15 ft   15 ft

15 ft

Volume = _____

Solve. Show your work.

> **Example**
>
> Steven fills a rectangular container measuring 17 centimeters by 14.5 centimeters by 12 centimeters with orange juice. How many liters and milliliters of orange juice are there in the container?
>
>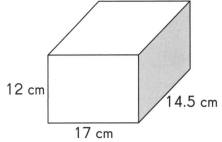
>
> Volume of orange juice in the container
> = 17 cm × 14.5 cm × 12 cm
> = 2,958 cm³
> = 2,958 mL
> = 2 L 958 mL
>
> The **capacity** of a container is the liquid volume of the container.
>
>

9. The base of a miniature rectangular fish tank measures 8 centimeters by 4.5 centimeters. The height of the tank is 6 centimeters. Find the capacity of the tank in liters and milliliters.

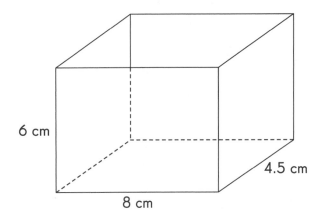

10. A rectangular container measures 6 centimeters by 3.5 centimeters by 12 centimeters. It is completely filled with water. How many liters and milliliters of water are there in the container?

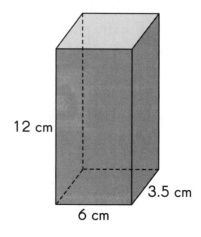

12 cm

3.5 cm

6 cm

11. A rectangular box measures 15 centimeters by 9 centimeters by 13 centimeters. Shannon uses the box to mix glue for her project. She fills the entire box with glue. How many liters and milliliters of glue are there in the box?

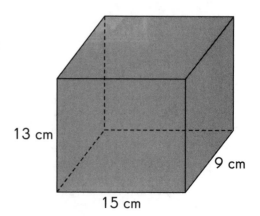

13 cm

9 cm

15 cm

12. A rectangular container is $\frac{1}{2}$-filled with water. How much water is needed to fill the container? After the container is filled, how much water must be poured out so that the container is $\frac{1}{3}$ full?

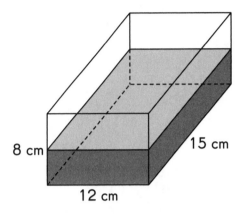

8 cm

15 cm

12 cm

13. A tank is $\frac{1}{2}$-filled with water. Some of the water is then poured into 8 small containers each with a capacity of 27 cubic centimeters. The tank is now $\frac{1}{4}$ full. What is the capacity of the tank?

14. A swimming pool, 25 meters wide, 50 meters long, and 12 meters deep, is $\frac{2}{3}$-filled with water. Its cross section is as shown below. How much water must be drained off so that the water level falls to 5 meters?

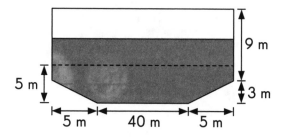

Answers

Chapter 8

Worksheet 1

1.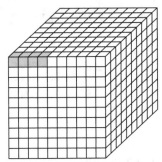

2. 0.017

3.

4.

5.

Ones	Tenths	Hundredths	Thousandths
	○○	○○○ ○○	○○○○ ○○○○

6. 1.423
7. 7
8. 540
9. 60
10. 37; 5
11. 0.107
12. 0.035
13. 0.393
14. 0.038
15. 0.007
16. 0.219
17. 0.035
18. 1.476
19. 2.005
20. 4.391
21. 3.056
22. 1.108

23. <u>2</u> ones and <u>8</u> tenths <u>1</u> hundredth <u>5</u> thousandths
24. <u>2</u> ones and <u>4</u> tenths <u>0</u> hundredths <u>9</u> thousandths
25. <u>7</u> ones and <u>0</u> tenths <u>9</u> hundredths <u>3</u> thousandths
26. <u>4</u> + <u>0.2</u> + <u>0.07</u> + <u>0.003</u>
27. <u>1</u> + <u>0.5</u> + <u>0.003</u>
28. <u>9</u> + <u>0.01</u> + <u>0.007</u>
29. 1; 6; 5
30. 5; 10; 100; 1000
31. 4; 7; 100; 8
32. 6; 9; 1000
33. 7; 5; 6; 1000
34. tenths
35. ones
36. thousandths
37. hundredths
38. 0.9
39. 0
40. 0.008
41. 6
42. 3 hundredths
43. tenths
44. thousandths
45. 7
46. 9.742
47. 5.814

Worksheet 2

1.

Ones	Tenths	Hundredths	Thousandths
0	1	0	8
0	1	2	0

Yes; Yes; No
<u>2</u> hundredths > <u>0</u> hundredths
0.12; 0.108

2. 3.9
3. 16.71
4. 105.67
5. 3.19
6. 99.89
7. 0.891
8. 133.2

9.

Ones	Tenths	Hundredths	Thousandths
4	8	5	7
4	8	5	2
4	8	5	4

Yes; Yes; Yes; No
<u>7</u> thousandths > <u>4</u> thousandths > <u>2</u> thousandths
4.852

10.

Ones	Tenths	Hundredths	Thousandths
5	2	7	3
5	2	9	1
5	2	4	8

Yes; Yes; No

<u>9</u> hundredths > <u>7</u> hundredths > <u>4</u> hundredths

5.291

11. (1.418) ~~1.814~~   **12.** (0.312) ~~0.37~~

13. (8.01) ~~8.181~~   **14.** (21.07) ~~27.1~~

15. (2.59) ~~2.95~~   **16.** (7.12) ~~7.22~~

17. (0.601) ~~0.641~~

18.

Ones	Tenths	Hundredths	Thousandths
3	5	8	6
0	3	1	4
3	5	6	7

No; No; No

<u>0.314</u>,   <u>3.567</u>,   <u>3.586</u>

least   greatest

19. 0.103,   0.131,   0.311

20. 0.15,   1.44,   5.14

21. 7.013,   7.033,   7.131

22. 9.009,   9.090,   9.900

23. 0.081,   0.118,   0.180

24. 3.639,   3.936,   3.963

25. 4.949,   9.449,   9.494

26. 0.62,   2.06,   6.02

27.

Ones	Tenths	Hundredths	Thousandths
2	3	9	6
1	4	3	1
2	3	0	2

No; No; No

<u>2.396</u>,   <u>2.302</u>,   <u>1.431</u>

greatest   least

28. 21.12,   12.21,   12.12

29. 0.110,   0.101,   0.011

30. 4.63,   4.36,   4.06

31.

0.15

32.

4.01

	Rounded to the Nearest		
Decimal	**Whole Number**	**Tenth**	**Hundredth**
33. 0.147	0	0.1	0.15
34. 2.564	3	2.6	2.56
35. 6.325	6	6.3	6.33

36. Answers vary.

Sample:

2.765, 2.766, 2.767, 2.768, or 2.769

37. 1.20

Worksheet 3

1. $\frac{4}{5}$

2. $5\frac{9}{10}$

3. $6\frac{1}{25}$

4. $\frac{47}{100}$

5. $\frac{9}{125}$

6. $7\frac{3}{200}$

7. $2\frac{109}{250}$

8. $2\frac{37}{1000}$

9. $4\frac{1}{125}$

10. $16\frac{3}{20}$

11. $\frac{377}{500}$

12. $\frac{1}{200}$

13. $4\frac{9}{25}$

14. $\frac{1}{50}$

15. $12\frac{3}{50}$

16. $11\frac{1}{125}$

17. $15\frac{13}{250}$

18. $17\frac{407}{500}$

19. $19\frac{3}{10}$

20. $9\frac{81}{200}$

21. $\frac{27}{250}$

22. $4\frac{7}{10}$

23. $\frac{3}{10}$

24. $1\frac{69}{200}$

25. $\frac{539}{1000}$

Chapter 9

Worksheet 1

1. 8; 8; 0.8

2. 9; 9; 0.9

3. 40; 40; 4.0

4. 16; 16; 1.6

5. 42; 42; 4.2

6. 0.6

7. 1.2

8. 2.4

9. 2.4

10. 4.0

11. 2.1

12. 4.5

13. <u>6</u> ones

14. <u>9</u> ones

15. <u>13</u> ones

16. <u>2</u> ones and <u>4</u> tenths

17. <u>3</u> ones and <u>7</u> tenths

18. <u>10</u> ones and <u>1</u> tenth

19. <u>24</u> tenths = <u>2</u> ones and <u>4</u> tenths

20. <u>35</u> tenths = <u>3</u> ones and <u>5</u> tenths

21. <u>48</u> tenths = <u>4</u> ones and <u>8</u> tenths

22. <u>12</u> ones and <u>8</u> tenths

23. <u>42</u> ones and <u>6</u> tenths

24. <u>18</u> ones and <u>9</u> tenths

25. 8 tenths × 5 = <u>40</u> tenths
<u>40</u> tenths = <u>4</u> ones and <u>0</u> tenths
2 ones × 5 = <u>10</u> ones
<u>4</u> ones + <u>10</u> ones = <u>14</u> ones
So, 2.8 × 5 = <u>14.0</u>.

26. 7 tenths × 3 = <u>21</u> tenths
<u>21</u> tenths = <u>2</u> ones and <u>1</u> tenth
4 ones × 3 = <u>12</u> ones
<u>2</u> ones + <u>12</u> ones = <u>14</u> ones
So, 4.7 × 3 = <u>14.1</u>.

27. 6 tenths × 4 = <u>24</u> tenths
<u>24</u> tenths = <u>2</u> ones and <u>4</u> tenths
5 ones × 4 = <u>20</u> ones
<u>2</u> ones + <u>20</u> ones = <u>22</u> ones
So, 5.6 × 4 = <u>22.4</u>.

28. 8 tenths × 7 = <u>56</u> tenths
<u>56</u> tenths = <u>5</u> ones and <u>6</u> tenths
6 ones × 7 = <u>42</u> ones
<u>5</u> ones + <u>42</u> ones = <u>47</u> ones
So, 6.8 × 7 = <u>47.6</u>.

29. 7 tenths × 4 = <u>28</u> tenths
<u>28</u> tenths = <u>2</u> ones and <u>8</u> tenths
3 ones × 4 = <u>12</u> ones
<u>2</u> ones + <u>12</u> ones = <u>14</u> ones
So, 3.7 × 4 = <u>14.8</u>.

30. 6 tenths × 6 = <u>36</u> tenths
<u>36</u> tenths = <u>3</u> ones and <u>6</u> tenths
1 one × 6 = <u>6</u> ones
<u>3</u> ones + <u>6</u> ones = <u>9</u> ones
So, 1.6 × 6 = <u>9.6</u>.

31. 22.4

32. 32.9

33. 13.8

34. 9; 9; 0.09

35. 8; 8; 0.08

36. 0.06

37. 0.12

38. 0.16

39. 0.05

40. 0.12

41. 0.18

42. 0.15

43. 0.20

44. <u>4</u> tenths <u>7</u> hundredths

45. <u>8</u> tenths <u>0</u> hundredths

46. <u>5</u> tenths <u>9</u> hundredths

47. <u>12</u> hundredths = <u>1</u> tenth <u>2</u> hundredths

48. <u>14</u> hundredths = <u>1</u> tenth <u>4</u> hundredths

49. <u>28</u> hundredths = <u>2</u> tenths <u>8</u> hundredths

50. <u>48</u> hundredths = <u>4</u> tenths <u>8</u> hundredths

51. <u>6</u> tenths + <u>2</u> tenths <u>4</u> hundredths
= <u>8</u> tenths <u>4</u> hundredths

52. <u>14</u> tenths + <u>2</u> tenths <u>1</u> hundredth
= <u>16</u> tenths <u>1</u> hundredth

53. <u>24</u> tenths + <u>1</u> tenth <u>6</u> hundredths
= <u>25</u> tenths <u>6</u> hundredths

54. <u>24</u> hundredths = <u>2</u> tenths <u>4</u> hundredths
So, 0.08 × 3 = <u>0.24</u>.

55. <u>35</u> hundredths = <u>3</u> tenths <u>5</u> hundredths
So, 0.05 × 7 = <u>0.35</u>.

56. 9 hundredths × 2 = <u>18</u> hundredths
<u>18</u> hundredths = <u>1</u> tenth <u>8</u> hundredths
4 tenths × 2 = <u>8</u> tenths
<u>1</u> tenth + <u>8</u> tenths = <u>9</u> tenths
<u>9</u> tenths = <u>0</u> ones and <u>9</u> tenths
So, 0.49 × 2 = <u>0.98</u>.

57. 5 hundredths $\times$ 3 = <u>15</u> hundredths
 <u>15</u> hundredths = <u>1</u> tenth <u>5</u> hundredths
 2 tenths $\times$ 3 = <u>6</u> tenths
 <u>1</u> tenth + <u>6</u> tenths = <u>7</u> tenths
 <u>7</u> tenths = <u>0</u> ones and <u>7</u> tenths
 So, 0.25 $\times$ 3 = <u>0.75</u>.

58. 3 hundredths $\times$ 4 = <u>12</u> hundredths
 <u>12</u> hundredths = <u>1</u> tenth <u>2</u> hundredths
 4 tenths $\times$ 4 = <u>16</u> tenths
 <u>1</u> tenth + <u>16</u> tenths = <u>17</u> tenths
 <u>17</u> tenths = <u>1</u> one and <u>7</u> tenths
 So, 0.43 $\times$ 4 = <u>1.72</u>.

59. 7 hundredths $\times$ 5 = <u>35</u> hundredths
 <u>35</u> hundredths = <u>3</u> tenths <u>5</u> hundredths
 6 tenths $\times$ 5 = <u>30</u> tenths
 <u>3</u> tenths + <u>30</u> tenths = <u>33</u> tenths
 <u>33</u> tenths = <u>3</u> ones and <u>3</u> tenths
 So, 0.67 $\times$ 5 = <u>3.35</u>.

60. 4.35

61. 9.44

62. 21.48

Worksheet 2

1. 12.8   2. 47.5
3. 3.6   4. 9.2
5. 34.5   6. 8.1
7. 64   8. 78
9. 7   10. 9
11. 53   12. 4
13. 3.75   14. 2.84
15. 16.93   16. 24.38
17. 7.36   18. 89.31
19. 13.9   20. 24.7
21. 8.4   22. 9.4
23. 72   24. 63
25. 8   26. 2
27. 4.81   28. 1.79
29. 24.35   30. 65.82
31. 10   32. 10
33. 10   34. 10

35. 1.208   36. 0.103
37. 0.305   38. 24.58
39. 4   40. 10
41. 15   42. 10
43. 10   44. 9
45. 10   46. 17
47. 6 $\times$ <u>7</u> $\times$ 10 = <u>42</u> $\times$ 10 = <u>420</u>
48. <u>8</u> $\times$ <u>12</u> $\times$ 10 = <u>96</u> $\times$ 10 = <u>960</u>
49. <u>11</u> $\times$ <u>5</u> $\times$ 10 = <u>55</u> $\times$ 10 = <u>550</u>
50. <u>16</u> $\times$ <u>18</u> $\times$ 10 = <u>288</u> $\times$ 10 = <u>2,880</u>
51. 630   52. 450
53. 480   54. 780
55. 750   56. 540
57. 137.5   58. 267.9
59. 47.2   60. 81.4
61. 578   62. 693
63. 38   64. 91
65. 1,492   66. 2,679
67. 385   68. 496
69. 4,670   70. 5,820
71. 400   72. 100
73. 100   74. 1,000
75. 100   76. 1,000
77. 0.369   78. 0.204
79. 0.048   80. 0.91
81. 5   82. 1,000
83. 9   84. 100
85. 100   86. 6
87. 1,000   88. 26
89. 3 $\times$ <u>8</u> $\times$ 1,000 = <u>24</u> $\times$ 1,000 = <u>24,000</u>
90. <u>7</u> $\times$ <u>11</u> $\times$ 100 = <u>77</u> $\times$ 100 = <u>7,700</u>
91. <u>12</u> $\times$ <u>6</u> $\times$ 1,000 = <u>72</u> $\times$ 1,000 = <u>72,000</u>
92. 32,000   93. 5,400
94. 30,000   95. 5,600
96. 91   97. 9,600
98. 900   99. 680

Worksheet 3

1. 3
2. 4
3. 3
4. 3
5. 5
6. 4
7. 4
8. 8
9. 8
10. 23
11. 5
12. 4
13. 7
14. 14
15. 9

16.
```
    2
 2) 4 . 6
    4
    0
```
Divide the ones by 2.
4 ones ÷ 2 = 2 ones

```
    2 . 3
 2) 4 . 6
    4
    0   6
        6
        0
```
Divide the tenths by 2.
6 tenths ÷ 2 = 3 tenths
So, 4.6 ÷ 2 = 2.3.

17.
```
    2
 3) 6 . 9
    6
    0
```
Divide the ones by 3.
6 ones ÷ 3 = 2 ones

```
    2 . 3
 3) 6 . 9
    6
    0   9
        9
        0
```
Divide the tenths by 3.
9 tenths ÷ 3 = 3 tenths
So, 6.9 ÷ 3 = 2.3.

18.
```
    2
 4) 8 . 4
    8
    0
```
Divide the ones by 4.
8 ones ÷ 4 = 2 ones

```
    2 . 1
 4) 8 . 4
    8
    0   4
        4
        0
```
Divide the tenths by 4.
4 tenths ÷ 4 = 1 tenth
So, 8.4 ÷ 4 = 2.1.

19.
```
    3 . 2
 2) 6 . 4
    6
    0   4
        4
        0
```

20.
```
    1 . 3
 3) 3 . 9
    3
    0   9
        9
        0
```

21.
```
    0 . 8
 3) 2 . 4
    0
    2   4
    2   4
        0
```

22.
```
    0 . 9
 6) 5 . 4
    0
    5   4
    5   4
        0
```

23.
```
    0 . 1
 7) 0 . 7
    0
    0   7
        7
        0
```

24.
```
    0 . 4
 8) 3 . 2
    0
    3   2
    3   2
        0
```

25. 4 ones = <u>3</u> ones and 10 tenths
    4 ones and 2 tenths
    = 3 ones and 10 tenths + 2 tenths
    = 3 ones and <u>12</u> tenths
    3 ones and <u>12</u> tenths 9 hundreds ÷ 3
    = <u>1</u> one and <u>4</u> tenths <u>3</u> hundredths

26. 3 ones = <u>2</u> ones and 10 tenths
    3 ones and 6 tenths
    = <u>2</u> ones and 10 tenths + <u>6</u> tenths
    = <u>2</u> ones and <u>16</u> tenths
    2 ones and <u>16</u> tenths <u>8</u> hundredths ÷ 2
    = <u>1</u> one and <u>8</u> tenths <u>4</u> hundredths

27. 5 tenths = <u>3</u> tenths 20 hundredths
    5 tenths 4 hundredths
    = <u>3</u> tenths 20 hundredths + <u>4</u> hundredths
    = <u>3</u> tenths <u>24</u> hundredths
    6 ones and <u>3</u> tenths <u>24</u> hundredths ÷ 3
    = <u>2</u> ones and <u>1</u> tenth <u>8</u> hundredths

28. 6 tenths = <u>4</u> tenths <u>20</u> hundredths
    6 tenths 4 hundredths
    = <u>4</u> tenths <u>20</u> hundredths + <u>4</u> hundredths
    = <u>4</u> tenths <u>24</u> hundredths
    4 ones and <u>4</u> tenths <u>24</u> hundredths ÷ 4
    = <u>1</u> one and <u>1</u> tenth <u>6</u> hundredths

29. 4 ones = <u>3</u> ones and <u>10</u> tenths
    9 tenths 5 hundredths
    = <u>8</u> tenths <u>10</u> hundredths + <u>5</u> hundredths
    = <u>8</u> tenths <u>15</u> hundredths
    3 ones and <u>18</u> tenths <u>15</u> hundredths ÷ 3
    = <u>1</u> one and <u>6</u> tenths <u>5</u> hundredths

30. 6 ones = <u>5</u> ones and <u>10</u> tenths
    6 ones and 5 tenths
    = <u>5</u> ones and <u>10</u> tenths + <u>5</u> tenths
    = <u>5</u> ones and <u>15</u> tenths
    5 ones and <u>15</u> tenths <u>5</u> hundredths ÷ 5
    = <u>1</u> one and <u>3</u> tenths <u>1</u> hundredth

31.

Divide the ones by 2.
4 ones ÷ 2 = <u>2</u> ones

Divide the tenths by 2.
5 tenths ÷ 2
= <u>2</u> tenths R <u>1</u> tenth
<u>1</u> tenth = <u>10</u> hundredths

Add the hundredths.
<u>10</u> hundredths +
<u>6</u> hundredths
= <u>16</u> hundredths

Divide the hundredths by 2.
<u>16</u> hundredths ÷ 2
= <u>8</u> hundredths
So, 4.56 ÷ 2 = <u>2.28</u>.

32.

```
      2
   _____
3 ) 6 . 5   7
    6
   ___
    0
```
Divide the ones by 3.
6 ones ÷ 3 = **2** ones

```
      2 . 1
   _____
3 ) 6 . 5   7
    6
   _____
    0   5
        3
       ___
        2
```
Divide the tenths by 3.
5 tenths ÷ 3
= **1** tenth R **2** tenths
2 tenths = **20** hundredths

```
      2 . 1
   _____
3 ) 6 . 5   7
    6
   _____
    0   5
        3
       ___
        2   7
```
Add the hundredths.
20 hundredths +
7 hundredths
= **27** hundredths

```
      2 . 1   9
   _____
3 ) 6 . 5   7
    6
   _____
    0   5
        3
       _____
        2   7
        2   7
           ___
            0
```
Divide the hundredths by 3.
27 hundredths ÷ 3
= **9** hundredths
So, 6.57 ÷ 3 = **2.19**.

33.

```
      2 . 1   8
   _____
4 ) 8 . 7   2
    8
   _____
    0   7
        4
       _____
        3   2
        3   2
           ___
            0
```

34.

```
      1 . 0   7
   _____
6 ) 6 . 4   2
    6
   _____
    0   4
        0
       _____
        4   2
        4   2
           ___
            0
```

35.

```
      2
   _____
2 ) 5 . 4   8
    4
   ___
    1
```
Divide the ones by 2.
5 ones ÷ 2
= **2** ones R **1** one

```
      2
   _____
2 ) 5 . 4   8
    4
   _____
    1   4
```
Regroup the remainder **1** one.
1 one = **10** tenths
Add the tenths.
10 tenths + **4** tenths
= **14** tenths

```
      2 . 7
   _____
2 ) 5 . 4   8
    4
   _____
    1   4
    1   4
       ___
        0
```
Divide the tenths by 2.
14 tenths ÷ 2 = **7** tenths

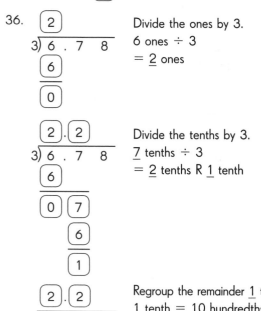

Divide the hundredths by 2.
8 hundredths ÷ 2
= 4 hundredths
So, 5.48 ÷ 2 = 2.74.

Divide the ones by 3.
6 ones ÷ 3
= 2 ones

Divide the tenths by 3.
7 tenths ÷ 3
= 2 tenths R 1 tenth

Regroup the remainder 1 tenth.
1 tenth = 10 hundredths
Add the hundredths.
10 hundredths +
8 hundredths
= 18 hundredths

Divide the hundredths by 3.
18 hundredths ÷ 3
= 6 hundredths
So, 6.78 ÷ 3 = 2.26.

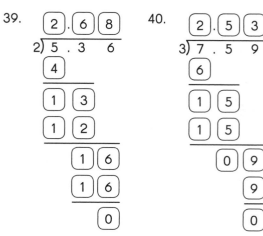

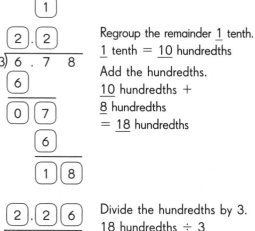

43. 0.24   44. 0.18
45. 2.28   46. 0.79
47. 1.88   48. 0.32
49. 0.18   50. 2.31
51. 1.57   52. 1.76
53. 0.14   54. 0.15
55. 0.97   56. 1.23
57. 0.66

58.

$$
\begin{array}{r}
0.66 \\
3\overline{)2.00} \\
0 \\
\hline
20 \\
18 \\
\hline
20 \\
18 \\
\hline
2
\end{array}
$$

2 ÷ 3 is about <u>0.7</u>.

59.

$$
\begin{array}{r}
0.85 \\
7\overline{)6.00} \\
0 \\
\hline
60 \\
56 \\
\hline
40 \\
35 \\
\hline
5
\end{array}
$$

6 ÷ 7 is about <u>0.9</u>.

60.

$$
\begin{array}{r}
1.16 \\
6\overline{)7.00} \\
6 \\
\hline
10 \\
6 \\
\hline
40 \\
36 \\
\hline
4
\end{array}
$$

7 ÷ 6 is about <u>1.2</u>.

61. 0.56

62. 1.14

63. 3.67

Worksheet 4

1. 0.137
2. 0.385
3. 3.62
4. 9.47
5. 64.5
6. 78.6

7. 0.09
8. 0.04
9. 0.284
10. 46.3
11. 0.095
12. 7.26
13. 10
14. 10
15. 10
16. 10
17. 30.9
18. 704
19. 0.5
20. 4.58
21. 3
22. 2
23. 280
24. 420
25. (60 ÷ <u>2</u>) ÷ 10 = <u>30</u> ÷ 10 = <u>3</u>
26. (120 ÷ <u>3</u>) ÷ 10 = <u>40</u> ÷ 10 = <u>4</u>
27. (<u>360</u> ÷ 4) ÷ 10 = <u>90</u> ÷ 10 = <u>9</u>
28. (<u>560</u> ÷ 8) ÷ 10 = <u>70</u> ÷ 10 = <u>7</u>
29. (<u>16</u> ÷ 8) ÷ 10 = <u>2</u> ÷ 10 = <u>0.2</u>
30. (<u>21</u> ÷ 7) ÷ 10 = <u>3</u> ÷ 10 = <u>0.3</u>
31. (<u>0.9</u> ÷ 3) ÷ 10 = <u>0.3</u> ÷ 10 = <u>0.03</u>
32. (<u>0.15</u> ÷ 5) ÷ 10 = <u>0.03</u> ÷ 10 = <u>0.003</u>
33. 0.02
34. 0.2
35. 0.3
36. 0.015
37. 0.006
38. 0.238
39. 0.473
40. 0.375
41. 0.984
42. 0.059
43. 0.027
44. 0.147
45. 0.258
46. 0.069
47. 0.038
48. 1.234
49. 6.101
50. 100
51. 1,000
52. 1,000
53. 100
54. 408
55. 205
56. 7
57. 852
58. 2
59. 3
60. 40
61. 6
62. 0.9
63. 2
64. 3
65. 180
66. 8
67. 0.8
68. 0.2
69. 0.02
70. 0.4
71. 0.09
72. 0.004
73. 0.005
74. 0.05
75. 0.02
76. 0.002
77. 0.015
78. 0.003
79. 0.008
80. 0.07

81. 0.15   82. 2.8
83. 5

Worksheet 5

1. 4 tenths is <u>less than</u> <u>5</u> tenths.
   12.459 → <u>12</u>
   12

2. 6 tenths is <u>greater than</u> <u>5</u> tenths.
   43.607 → <u>44</u>
   44

3. 9 tenths is <u>greater than</u> <u>5</u> tenths.
   28.910 → <u>29</u>
   29

4. 4 hundredths is <u>less than</u> <u>5</u> hundredths.
   6.341 → <u>6.3</u>
   6.3

5. 5 hundredths is <u>equal to</u> <u>5</u> hundredths.
   17.251 → <u>17.3</u>
   17.3

6. 0 hundredths is <u>less than</u> <u>5</u> hundredths.
   39.908 → <u>39.9</u>
   39.9

7. 7 hundredths is <u>greater than</u> <u>5</u> hundredths.
   18.472 → <u>18.5</u>
   18.5

8. 6 thousandths is <u>greater than</u> <u>5</u> thousandths.
   16.016 → <u>16.02</u>
   16.02

9. 5 thousandths is <u>equal to</u> <u>5</u> thousandths.
   24.005 → <u>24.01</u>
   24.01

10. 6 thousandths is <u>greater than</u> <u>5</u> thousandths.
    45.076 → <u>45.08</u>
    45.08

11. 1.62 → <u>2</u> ; 3.39 → <u>3</u>
    <u>2</u> + <u>3</u> = <u>5</u>
    5

12. 4.53 → <u>5</u> ; 0.82 → <u>1</u>
    <u>5</u> + <u>1</u> = <u>6</u>
    6

13. 7.49 → <u>7</u> ; 2.39 → <u>2</u>
    <u>7</u> + <u>2</u> = <u>9</u>
    9

14. 18.57 → <u>19</u> ; 9.98 → <u>10</u>
    <u>19</u> + <u>10</u> = <u>29</u>
    29

15. 4.67 → <u>5</u> ; 0.88 → <u>1</u>
    <u>5</u> + <u>1</u> = <u>6</u>
    6

16. 7.39 → <u>7.4</u> ; 2.91 → <u>2.9</u>
    <u>7.4</u> − <u>2.9</u> = <u>4.5</u>
    4.5

17. 2.4   18. 7.7

19. 8.9   20. 22.7

21. 3.51 → <u>4</u>
    <u>4</u> × <u>7</u> = <u>28</u>
    28

22. 96   23. 176

24. 216   25. 351

26. 4.54 → <u>4.5</u>
    <u>4.5</u> × <u>6</u> = <u>27</u>
    27

27. 100.1   28. 152.1

29. 31.52 → <u>32</u>
    <u>32</u> ÷ <u>8</u> = <u>4</u>
    4

30. 8   31. 9

32. 37.24 → <u>37.2</u>
    <u>37.2</u> ÷ <u>6</u> = <u>6.2</u>

33. 2.7   34. 7.3

Worksheet 6

1. 3.2 cm → <u>3</u> cm
   <u>3</u> × <u>4</u> = <u>12</u> cm
   The total length is about <u>12</u> centimeters.

2. 7.57 cm → 8 cm
   8 × 6 = 48 cm
   The total length is about <u>48</u> centimeters.

3. 78.65 →
   6 × <u>12</u> = <u>72</u>
   6 × <u>13</u> = <u>78</u>
   6 × <u>14</u> = <u>84</u>
   <u>78.65</u> is nearer to 78.
   Since 6 × <u>13</u> = 78, each child gets about
   $<u>13</u>.

4. 65 →
   4 × <u>15</u> = <u>60</u>
   4 × <u>16</u> = <u>64</u>
   4 × <u>17</u> = <u>68</u>
   <u>64</u> is nearer to 65.
   Since 4 × <u>16</u> = <u>64</u>, the length of each cut
   part of the rope is about <u>16</u> meters.

5. $6.80 → $7
   $4.50 → $5
   $7.75 → $8
   $6.80 + $4.50 + $7.75
   ≈ $7 + $5 + $8 = $20
   Yes, Jennifer has enough money to buy all three items.

6. 2.17 liters × 9 = 19.53 liters
   ≈ 20 liters
   The capacity of the larger bucket is about 20 liters.

7. 15.67 mi − 8.92 mi = 6.75 mi
   ≈ 7 mi
   The distance between the café and the school is about 7 miles.

8. 9.33 min − 7.5 min = 1.83 min
   ≈ 2 min
   He must shave about 2 minutes off his best time to achieve his goal.

Chapter 10

Worksheet 1

1. 34	2. 34
3. 66	4. 66
5. 18	6. 55
7. 63	8. 90
9. 70	10. 80
11. 40; 40	12. 79; 79
13. 46; 46	14. 1; 1
15. 8; 8	16. 9; 9
17. $\frac{21}{100}$	18. $\frac{63}{100}$
19. $\frac{9}{100}$	20. $\frac{3}{100}$
21. 37; 0.37	22. 94; 0.94
23. 5; 0.05	24. 9; 0.09
25. $\frac{9}{25}$	26. $\frac{3}{20}$
27. $\frac{18}{25}$	28. $\frac{9}{50}$
29. 42; $\frac{21}{50}$	30. 75; $\frac{3}{4}$
31. 8; $\frac{2}{25}$	32. 5; $\frac{1}{20}$

		Percent	Decimal
33.	7 out of 100	7	0.07
34.	4 out of 10	40	0.4
35.	9 out of 10	90	0.9

		Decimal	Fraction
36.	0%	0	0
37.	8%	0.08	$\frac{2}{25}$
38.	33%	0.33	$\frac{33}{100}$
39.	74%	0.74	$\frac{37}{50}$
40.	100%	1.0	$\frac{100}{100}$

		Percent	Fraction
41.	0	0	0
42.	0.7	70	$\frac{7}{10}$
43.	0.44	44	$\frac{11}{25}$
44.	0.73	73	$\frac{73}{100}$
45.	1	100	1

46. 45; 55   47. 30; 70
48. 35; 65   49. 76; 24

50.

51.

Worksheet 2

1. 55; 55	2. 94; 94
3. 60; 60	4. 75; 75

5. 68; 68

6. $\frac{31}{50}$; 1; $\frac{31}{50}$; 100; 62

7. $\frac{9}{20}$; 1; $\frac{9}{20}$; 100; 45

8. 22; 22

9. 17; 17

10. 25; 25

11. 53; 53

12. 5; 65; 65

13. 4; 36; 36

14. 1 unit ⟶ 4%

    7 units ⟶ 28%

    Homework completed = 28%

    Homework not completed = 72%

15. 5 units ⟶ 100%

    1 unit ⟶ 20%

    4 units ⟶ 80%

    a. Kenneth did 80% of his homework.

    b. 20% of his homework was left undone.

16. $\frac{18}{25} \times 100\% = 72\%$

    $100\% - 72\% = 28\%$

    28% of Ahmad's land was planted with orange trees.

17. $\frac{1}{4} + \frac{1}{5} = \frac{9}{20}$

    Fraction of journey completed = $\frac{9}{20}$

    20 units ⟶ 100%

    1 unit ⟶ 5%

    11 units ⟶ 55%

    Percent of journey not completed = 55%

18. $\frac{1}{3} + \frac{5}{12} = \frac{3}{4}$

    Fraction of fruits that were apples and oranges = $\frac{3}{4}$

    4 units ⟶ 100%

    1 unit ⟶ 25%

    Percent of fruits that were pears = 25%

19. $\frac{1}{2} + \frac{1}{4} = \frac{3}{4}$

    Fraction of pizza given away = $\frac{3}{4}$

    4 units ⟶ 100%

    1 unit ⟶ 25%

    Percent of pizza left = 25%

Worksheet 3

1. 0.3; 15

2. 0.4; 24

3. $\frac{70}{100}$; 150; 105

4. $\frac{45}{100}$; 320; 144

5. **Method 1:**

   40% of 480 eggs = $\frac{40}{100} \times 480$

   = 192

   192 eggs hatched.

   Method 2:

   100% ⟶ 480 eggs

   1% ⟶ 4.8 eggs

   40% ⟶ 192 eggs

   192 eggs hatched.

6. **Method 1:**

   60% of $850 = $\frac{60}{100} \times \$850$

   = $510

   Mrs. Smith spent $510 on the gifts.

   Method 2:

   100% ⟶ $850

   1% ⟶ $8.50

   60% ⟶ $510

   Mrs. Smith spent $510 on the gifts.

7. a. 100% − 15% = 85%

   85% of the meat was kept in the refrigerator.

   b. **Method 1:**

   85% × 240 kg

   = $\frac{85}{100} \times 240$ kg

   = 204 kg

   204 kilograms of meat were kept in the refrigerator.

   Method 2:

   100% ⟶ 240

   1% ⟶ 2.4

   85% ⟶ 204

   204 kilograms of meat were kept in the refrigerator.

8. a. 100% − (55% + 22%) = 23%

   23% of the students were Chinese.

   b. 23% of 800

   = $\frac{23}{100} \times 800 = 184$

   184 of the students were Chinese.

9. $100\% - (45\% + 42\%) = 13\%$

13% of $\$2,000 = \dfrac{13}{100} \times \$2,000 = \$260$

Mr. Anderson saved $260.

Worksheet 4

1. 4% of $\$1,600 = \dfrac{4}{100} \times \$1,600 = \$64$

Mr. Taylor will get $64 after 1 year.

2. 6% of $\$1,200 = \dfrac{6}{100} \times \$1,200 = \$72$

a. Mrs. Benjamin will get $72 in interest after 1 year.

b. $\$1,200 + \$72 = \$1,272$

Mrs. Benjamin will have $1,272 in the bank after 1 year.

3. 5% of $\$800 = \dfrac{5}{100} \times \$800 = \$40$

Benny paid $40 in sales tax.

4. a. 5% of $\$1,500 = \dfrac{5}{100} \times \$1,500$

$= \$75$

Lisa paid $75 in sales tax.

b. $\$1,500 + \$75 = \$1,575$

Lisa paid $1,575 in total.

5. 15% of $\$1,200 = \dfrac{15}{100} \times \$1,200$

$= \$180$

The dollar amount of the discount was $180.

6. 20% of $\$4,200 = \dfrac{20}{100} \times \$4,200$

$= \$840$

The dollar amount of the discount was $840.

a. $\$4,200 - \$840 = \$3,360$

The discounted price for the piano was $3,360.

b. 5% of $\$3,360 = \dfrac{5}{100} \times \$3,360$

$= \$168$

She paid $168 in sales tax.

Chapter 11

Worksheet 1

Points Scored by Students

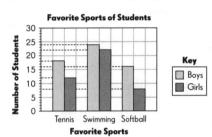

1. Carrie
2. Flora
3. 5
4. Ben
5. 5
6. 5

Favorite Sports of Students

7. 18
8. Swimming; 22
9. Swimming
10. Softball
11. 42
12. 58

Fruits Picked

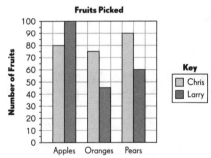

13. 245
14. Chris; 40
15. Pears; Apples
16. Oranges
17. 15
18. 60

Worksheet 2

1. P ($\underline{4}$, $\underline{8}$)
2. Q ($\underline{8}$, $\underline{4}$)
3. R ($\underline{0}$, $\underline{5}$)
4. S ($\underline{5}$, $\underline{0}$)

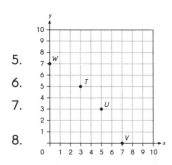

5.

6.

7.

8.

9. 3   10. 3.75   11. 20   12. 12

13. 1.875

14. Week 3   15. 8   16. 70

17. 36; 48   18. Jacob; 10

Worksheet 3

1.

	Socks	Ties	Combinations
1	red	blue	red/blue
2	black		black/blue
3	green		green/blue
4	red	brown	red/brown
5	black		black/brown
6	green		green/brown

6

2. 4; 2

3. a.

Drinks	Food	Combinations
coffee	cheese	coffee/cheese
	biscuits	coffee/biscuits
	fruit	coffee/fruit
tea	cheese	tea/cheese
	biscuits	tea/biscuits
	fruit	tea/fruit

b. There are six combinations in all.

4. a. 4 × 5 = 20
   b. 5 × 6 = 30
   c. 4 × 6 = 24

Worksheet 4

1. (H, T), (H, H), (T, H), (T, T); 4

2. $\frac{1}{2}$ 3. $\frac{1}{4}$

4. $\frac{1}{4}$

5. (H, 1), (H, 2), (H, 3), (H, 4), (H, 5), (H, 6), (T, 1), (T, 2), (T, 3), (T, 4), (T, 5), (T, 6); 12

6. $\frac{1}{4}$ 7. $\frac{1}{3}$

8. $\frac{1}{4}$ 9. $\frac{9}{20}$

10. $\frac{11}{20}$

11.

Number	Jenny's outcomes	Experimental probability	Trish's outcomes	Experimental probability
1	8	$\frac{8}{45}$	7	$\frac{7}{45}$
2	9	$\frac{1}{5}$	8	$\frac{8}{45}$
3	8	$\frac{8}{45}$	8	$\frac{8}{45}$
4	6	$\frac{2}{15}$	7	$\frac{7}{45}$
5	5	$\frac{1}{9}$	6	$\frac{2}{15}$
6	9	$\frac{1}{5}$	9	$\frac{1}{5}$

12. Answers vary.

Sample: Harris spins the spinner 100 times.

Number of times the spinner lands on:

Red   52

Green   25

Yellow   23

Chapter 12

Worksheet 1

1. m∠EXA = 120°
   m∠AXC = 60°
   $\overleftrightarrow{EC}$ is a line because
   m∠EXA + m∠AXC = 180°.

2. $m\angle a = \underline{119°}$
   $m\angle b = 180° - \underline{119°} = \underline{61°}$

3. $m\angle a = \underline{124°}$
   $m\angle b = \underline{180°} - \underline{124°} = \underline{56°}$

4. $m\angle t = \underline{180°} - 66° = \underline{114°}$

5. $m\angle AOC = \underline{180°} - \underline{134°} = \underline{46°}$

6. $m\angle x = \underline{40°}$
   $m\angle y = 90° - m\angle x$
   $ = 90° - \underline{40°}$
   $ = \underline{50°}$

7. $m\angle x = \underline{28°}$
   $m\angle y = 90° - m\angle x$
   $ = 90° - \underline{28°}$
   $ = \underline{62°}$

8. $m\angle DBC = \underline{90°} - \underline{58°} = \underline{32°}$

9. $m\angle CBD = \underline{90°} - \underline{27°} = \underline{63°}$

10. $m\angle y + \underline{131°} = 180°$
    $m\angle y = \underline{180°} - \underline{131°} = \underline{49°}$

11. $m\angle y + \underline{164°} = 180°$
    $m\angle y = \underline{180°} - \underline{164°} = \underline{16°}$

12. $m\angle x = 90° - 25° - 18° = \underline{47°}$

13. $m\angle x = 180° - 45° - 34° = \underline{101°}$

14.

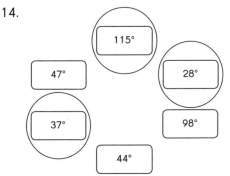

Worksheet 2

1. $m\angle \underline{SOP} + m\angle \underline{POQ} + m\angle \underline{QOR} + m\angle \underline{ROS}$
   $= 360°$

2. $m\angle POQ + m\angle QOR + m\angle ROS + m\angle SOP$
   $= \underline{100°} + \underline{80°} + \underline{100°} + \underline{80°}$
   $= \underline{360°}$

3. $m\angle s = \underline{122°}$
   $m\angle t = 360° - m\angle s$
   $ = 360° - \underline{122°}$
   $ = \underline{238°}$

4. $m\angle s = \underline{55°}$
   $m\angle t = 360° - m\angle s$
   $ = 360° - \underline{55°}$
   $ = \underline{305°}$

5. $m\angle x = \underline{360°} - 115° = \underline{245°}$

6. $m\angle PQR = \underline{360°} - \underline{245°} = \underline{115°}$

7. $m\angle x = 180° - 98° = 82°$
   $m\angle y = 180° - 82° = 98°$
   $m\angle z = 180° - 98° = 82°$

8. $m\angle x = 360° - 154° - 42° - 108° = 56°$

9. $m\angle x = 180° - 28° - 115° = 37°$

10.

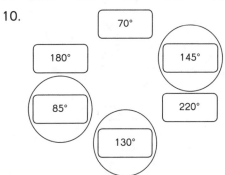

Worksheet 3

1. $m\angle \underline{AXB} = m\angle \underline{DXC}$
   $m\angle \underline{AXD} = m\angle \underline{BXC}$

2.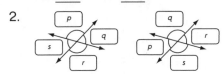

3. $m\angle \underline{w} = m\angle \underline{y}$
   $m\angle \underline{x} = m\angle \underline{z}$

4. $m\angle YOZ = 180° - 32° = \underline{148°}$
   $m\angle WOX = m\angle YOZ = \underline{148°}$

5. $m\angle AOD = 180° - 143° = \underline{37°}$
   $m\angle COD = m\angle AOB = \underline{143°}$
   $m\angle BOC = m\angle AOD = \underline{37°}$

6. $m\angle x = 360° - 136° - 42° - 90° = \underline{92°}$

7. $m\angle AOD = 86° - 28° = 58°$
   $m\angle x = m\angle AOD = 58°$

8. $m\angle UOV = 58° - 28° = 30°$
   $m\angle TOU = 100° - 30° = 70°$
   $m\angle SOT = 180° - 58° - 70° = 52°$

Chapter 13

Worksheet 1

1. True

2. True

3. False

4. True

5. False

6. ✔

7. ◯

8. ◯

9. True   10. False

11. True   12. True

13. ✔   14. ✔

15. ◯   16. True

17. True   18. ✔

19. ◯   20. ✔

21. True   22. False

23. False   24. ✔

25. ◯   26. ✔

27. False   28. True

29. ◯   30. ✔

31. ◯   32. False

33. True   34. ◯

35. ✔   36. ◯

Worksheet 2

1. True   2. True

3. False   4. True

5. 62°   6. 110°

7. 37°   8. 37°

9. 32°

10. a. 45°   b. 45°

11. Answers vary. Sample: *ABD*; *ADB*; *BAD*

12. False   13. True

14. True

15. *PQS*; *QPS*; *QSP*

16. *QRS*; *QSR*; *SQR*

17. *PRS*; *RSP*; *SPR*

18. *SPR*; *PRS*; *QSP*; *QSR*

19. True   20. True

21. Answers vary. Accept any two angle measures with a sum of 100°.

22. Answers vary. Accept any two angle measures with a sum of 100°.

23. Answers vary. Accept any two angle measures with a sum of 100°.

Worksheet 3

1. 22   2. 155

3. 45   4. 50

5. $m\angle FEG = \underline{51}°$, $m\angle EFG = \underline{51}°$

6. 64   7. 77

8. a. $m\angle C = 55°$

     b. $m\angle DAC = 35°$

9. a. $m\angle C = 37.5°$

     b. $m\angle ADB = 62.5°$

10. $m\angle b = 60°$ 11. $m\angle c = 60°$

12. $m\angle d = 120°$; $m\angle e = 120°$; $m\angle f = 120°$

13. $m\angle g = 30°$ 14. $m\angle h = 83°$

15. $m\angle i = 308°$; $m\angle j = 284°$

16. $m\angle k = 222°$ 17. $m\angle l = 93°$

Worksheet 4

1. 5   2. 7

3. 3   4. 12

5. 10   6. 8

7. Yes   8. Yes

9. Yes

10. 2 in. + 3 in. = 5 in.

     5 in. = 5 in.

     3 in. + 5 in. = 8 in.

     8 in. > 2 in.

     2 in. + 5 in. = 7 in.

     7 in. > 3 in.

     This triangle cannot be formed. The sum of one pair of the sides is equal to the third side.

11. 4 cm + 5 cm = 9 cm

     9 cm < 10 cm

     5 cm + 10 cm = 15 cm

     15 cm > 4 cm

     4 cm + 10 cm = 14 cm

     14 cm > 5 cm

     This triangle cannot be formed. The sum of one pair of the sides is less than the third side.

12. 6 cm + 7 cm = 13 cm

     13 cm > 8 cm

     7 cm + 8 cm = 15 cm

     15 cm > 6 cm

     6 cm + 8 cm = 14 cm

     14 cm > 7 cm

     This triangle can be formed.

13. $AB + BC = 5$ in. $+ 6$ in.
    $= 11$ in.
    $AB + BC > AC$
    11 in. $> AC$

    So, AC is greater than 4 inches and less than 11 inches. The possible lengths of AC are 5 inches, 6 inches, 7 inches, 8 inches, 9 inches, and 10 inches.

14. $XY + YZ = 11$ cm $+ 15$ cm
    $= 26$ cm
    $XY + YZ > XZ$
    26 cm $> XZ$

    So, XZ is greater than 20 centimeters and less than 26 centimeters. The possible lengths of XZ are 21 centimeters, 22 centimeters, 23 centimeters, 24 centimeters, and 25 centimeters.

Worksheet 5

1. False
2. False
3. True
4. True
5. ◯
6. ✔
7. $m\angle b = 42°$; $m\angle c = 138°$
8. $m\angle d = 100°$; $m\angle e = 42°$
9. $m\angle f = 87°$; $m\angle g = 45°$
10. $m\angle h = 62°$; $m\angle i = 42°$
11. True
12. False
13. True
14. True
15. True
16. ✔
17. ◯
18. $m\angle b = 32°$; $m\angle c = 32°$
19. $m\angle d = 28°$; $m\angle e = 124°$
20. $m\angle f = 28°$; $m\angle g = 62°$;
    $m\angle h = 118°$
21. $m\angle i = 36°$; $m\angle j = 54°$
22. False
23. False
24. False
25. False
26. False
27. ◯
28. ✔
29. $m\angle y = 38°$
30. $m\angle p = 96°$; $m\angle q = 33°$;
    $m\angle r = 19°$
31. $m\angle p = 62°$
32. $m\angle q = 59°$
33. $m\angle r = 44°$; $m\angle s = 46°$

34. $m\angle t = 61°$; $m\angle u = 58°$
35. $m\angle v = 142°$; $m\angle w = 52°$

Chapter 14

Worksheet 1

1. Answers vary. Sample:

2. (Triangle) (Square) Rectangle
   Parallelogram Pentagon Hexagon

3.

4.
   ◯ ◯ ✔ ◯ ◯ ◯ ✔

5. Rectangular prism
   Pentagonal prism
   Triangular prism
   Octagonal prism
   Hexagonal prism

	Type of prism	Number of faces	Number of edges	Number of vertices
6.	Rectangular	6	12	8
7.	Pentagonal	7	15	10
8.	Triangular	5	9	6
9.	Octagonal	10	24	16
10.	Hexagonal	8	18	12

11.

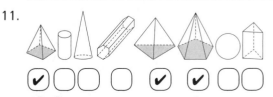

✔ ◯ ◯ ✔ ✔ ◯ ◯

12.

Triangular pyramid

Rectangular pyramid

Pentagonal pyramid

Hexagonal pyramid

Octagonal pyramid

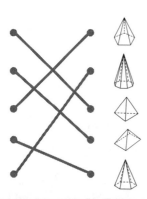

Type of pyramid	Number of faces	Number of edges	Number of vertices
13. Triangular	4	6	4
14. Rectangular	5	8	5
15. Pentagonal	6	10	6
16. Hexagonal	7	12	7
17. Octagonal	9	16	9

18.

19. Answers vary.
Sample:

20.

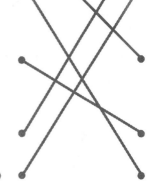

1.

2.

 green
red

3. (Circle)   Triangle   Square
   Rectangle   Parallelogram

4. (Circle)   Triangle   Square
   (Rectangle)   Pentagon

5.

6.

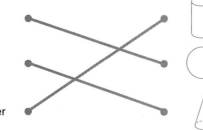

7.

Sphere

Cone

Cylinder

Chapter 15

Worksheet 1

1. 12   2. 11   3. 9   4. 5
5. 8   6. 10   7. 5   8. 10

9. Answers vary.
Sample:

10. Answers vary.
Sample:

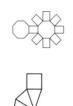

Worksheet 2

1.
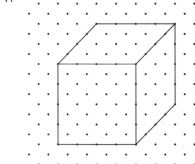

2.
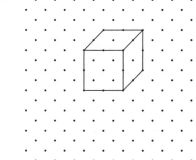

3.
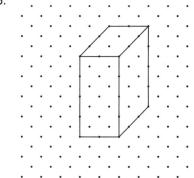

4.
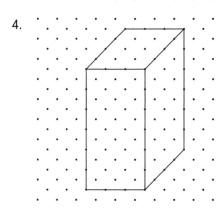

5.
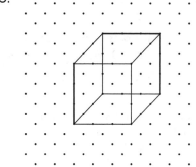

6.
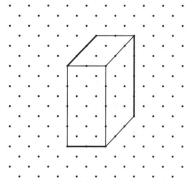

7.
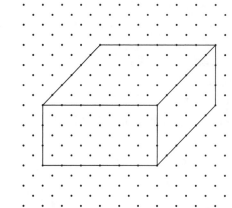

Worksheet 3

1. 294 cm²   2. 1,176 in.²

3. 1,536 cm²   4. 166 cm²

5. 460 in.²   6. 1,122 in.²

7. 278 m²   8. 576 cm²

9. 546 in.²

10. (110 cm × 85 cm + 85 cm × 40 cm
    + 110 cm × 40 cm) × 2 = 34,300 cm²

    The surface area of the cupboard is
    34,300 square centimeters.

11. 96 cm × 78 cm + (78 cm × 34 cm + 96 cm × 34 cm) × 2 = 19,320 cm²

The surface area of the outside of the cabinet without the cover is 19,320 square centimeters.

12. (12 ft × 7 ft + 8.5 ft × 7 ft) × 2 − 2 × 6.5 ft = 274 ft²

The surface area of the walls in the room is 274 square feet.

Worksheet 4

1. 7
2. 8
3. 9
4. 9
5. 10
6. 11
7. 13
8. 16
9. 7; 13; C; D
10. 12; 19; F; E
11. 5; 3; 4; 60; 4; 2; 3; 24; G; H
12. 3; 3; 3; 27; 5; 5; 4; 100; K; M

Worksheet 5

1. 512 cm³
2. 17,010 cm³
3. 2,197 m³
4. 11,400 m³
5. 23,712 in.³
6. 729 in.³
7. 12,852 ft³
8. 3,375 ft³
9. 8 cm × 4.5 cm × 6 cm
   = 216 cm³
   = 216 mL
   = 0 L 216 mL

   The capacity of the fish tank is 0 liters 216 milliliters.

10. 6 cm × 3.5 cm × 12 cm
    = 252 cm³
    = 252 mL
    = 0 L 252 mL

    There are 0 liters 252 milliliters of water in the container.

11. 15 cm × 9 cm × 13 cm
    = 1,755 cm³
    = 1,755 mL
    = 1 L 755 mL

    There are 1 liter 755 milliliters of glue in the box.

12. $\frac{1}{2}$ × 12 cm × 15 cm × 8 cm
    = 720 cm³ = 720 mL

    720 milliliters of water are needed to fill up the container.

    $\frac{1}{3}$ × 12 cm × 15 cm × 8 cm
    = 480 cm³ = 480 mL

    720 mL × 2 − 480 mL = 960 mL

    960 milliliters of water must be poured out so that the container is $\frac{1}{3}$ full.

13. $\frac{1}{2} - \frac{1}{4} = \frac{1}{4}$

    8 × 27 cm³ = 216 cm³

    $\frac{1}{4}$ ➙ 216 cm³

    $\frac{4}{4}$ ➙ 216 cm³ × 4 = 864 cm³

    The capacity of the tank is 864 cubic centimeters.

14. Current volume of water

    = $\frac{2}{3}$ × 50 m × 25 m × 12 m − 5 m × 3 m × 25 m

    = 9,625 m³

    Final volume of water
    = 50 m × 25 m × 5 m − 5 m × 3 m × 25 m
    = 5,875 m³
    9,625 m³ − 5,875 m³
    = 3,750 m³
    3,750 cubic meters of water must be drained off.